D1107420

LEXICON OF
HERBS

Growing • Cuisine • Cosmetics • Health Effects

Andrea Rausch
Brigitte Lotz

REBO
PUBLISHERS

© 2004 Rebo International b.v., Lisse, The Netherlands

Text: Andrea Rausch
Photographs: Brigitte Lotz
Typesetting: AdAm Studio, Prague, The Czech Republic
Cover design: AdAm Studio, Prague, The Czech Republic

Translation: Agentura Slůně, Ostrava for Agentura Abandon, Prague, The Czech Republic
Proofreading: Emily Sands, Laura Grec, Eva Munk

ISBN 90 366 1692 1

Contents:

Introduction

THE HISTORY OF GROWING HERBS

The knowledge and study of herbs and spices is nearly as old as mankind itself. Many cuttings and seeds from Mediterranean plants were transported across the Alps by the Romans and missionary monks, enriching their herb gardens. Later, many new variants emerged, thanks to crossbreeding. This involved not only Charlemague but also people such as the Abbess Hildegard of Bingen, who amassed a treasure trove of plants in convent gardens and applied the knowledge of how to grow them. Their knowledge endured and was added to by successive generations. However, due to the technical revolution and therapies of the 20th century, the preparation and use of herbs dwindled in popularity.

Nowadays, people long for a return to healthful, natural foods and therapies. What could be more healthful and natural than treating oneself with herbal aromas and therapeutic plants? We have described in detail the most important spices and herbs so that you can grow and harvest them successfully. Besides information regarding treatment with herbs (herbalism), you can also find several recipes that show you how many uses each herb and spice has.

WHAT SHOULD AN HERB GARDEN LOOK LIKE?

You may set up your herb garden in any way that pleases you. It does not matter if it is a full-sized herb bed for the whole family, a small garden on your balcony, or even a small garden on your window ledge. The advantage of growing herbs in small pots indoors is that you can preserve plants that are affected by cold weather, such as basil and summer savory. Perennial herbs such as thyme and hyssop can be easily integrated into other groups of perennials. A spiral of herbs can be very practical in that you can grow many plants in a small space. It is important to note that herbs such as parsley, chervil, lovage, and peppermint should be grown on the cooler, northern side, while plants such as thyme, marjoram, sage, and rosemary should be grown on the upper, sunny, and drier side. Herbs used for cooking are most practically grown in a place close to your kitchen.

SEEDS OR SEEDLINGS?

You can buy many herbs as seeds or seedlings from nurseries, markets, or through the mail. Some of them are easily propagated. You can divide them, snip cuttings, or harvest seeds. Herbs that need warmth, such as basil or rosemary, should be germinated indoors. Spread the seeds of herbs that do not need to be started early directly on the beds. Of course it all depends on price and quantity. Seeds are cheaper than seedlings; however, sometimes all you need is just one seedling. In the description of each herb, you will find the exact process you should follow to grow it successfully.

TIPS FOR THE CARE AND FEEDING OF HERBS

You can grow frost-resistant herbs throughout the year in pots. However, the most ideal seasons are spring and fall. Herbs that need warmth should be grown outdoors only when the risk of frost is not great. The bed should be well prepared. Hard soil should be mixed with sand and compost. You can improve poor soil by mixing it with a nutritious compost. Adding compost or organic fertilizers to the soil in spring ensures that the plants receive sufficient nutrition. If necessary, after the harvest you can add liquid fertilizers (liquids made for plants or prepared mixtures) again in summer.

Beware of overfertilization; overfertilized herbs grow faster, but are less aromatic.

Many plants that like sunny places become dry and need watering, especially those grown in pots, because they do not get any moisture from the earth. These should be fed with a liquid fertilizer every 4 weeks in summer. Thin mulch spread over the soil protects them from both dryness and weeds. You can prune some herbs in fall, and again in spring.

PROTECTING THE PLANTS

You can avoid plant damage and diseases by using optimal varieties and choosing the right place for them. The intense aroma of herbs often repels harmful insects. However, if insects do attack the plants, use environmentally sound methods to get rid of them: cut off the damaged parts of the plants, pick off the insects, introduce insect traps, or repot the herbs. If severe damage occurs, reach immediately for chemical compounds (e.g., potassium oxide).

MIXTURE TO HELP FIGHT PLANT-LICE: put 2 pounds of fresh nettles or half a pound of dried nettles into 10 quarts of water. Leave to ferment for about 2 weeks, stirring every day.

To pour over the plants, dilute the mixture in water at a ratio of 1:10; to spray the plants, dilute in a ratio of 1:20. If the smell of the mixture on your balcony or terrace offends you, you can prepare an unfermented mixture. Put the nettles in cold water, but do not leave to ferment. The unfermented mixture can be used in 1 or 2 days to spray the plants.

MIXTURE TO HELP FIGHT MILDEW, RUST, AND SCALE: put half a pound of fresh cabbage or 1 ounce of dried cabbage into 10 quarts of water and leave to ferment for 24 hours. Then boil for 30 minutes. Let it cool, then mix with water at a ratio of 1:5. It is best to use the formula in the morning together with the moonwort infusion below.

MOONWORT INFUSION TO HELP FIGHT APHIDS AND MITES: mix half a pound of fresh moonwort or 1 ounce dried moonwort with 10 quarts boiling water. Boil for 10 to 15 minutes, remove from heat, and allow the liquid to cool. Then mix with water at a ratio of 1:3.

Herbs are a fine source of nectar for bees and butterflies. They also attract helpful insects such as hoverflies, green lacewings, and ladybugs, which are the natural predators of larval insects.

CULTIVATION

Choosing a location for a plant depends on the other plants already there. Plants influence one another in both positive and negative ways through their aroma, root systems, and effectiveness in defending themselves against pests. Here are some examples of plants that can be grown close to each other:

• Brussels sprouts protect bean plants from aphids. Also, lavender protects roses against aphids.

• Caraway, cress, and horseradish improve the taste of potatoes.

• Dill, fennel, caraway, and coriander grow especially well next to cucumbers, carrots, and onions.

• Peppermint, sage, and thyme repel cabbage butterflies.

• However, onions and similar species should not be grown near beans. Similarly, parsley does not grow well near lettuce.

WHAT MAKES HERBS SO GOOD FOR YOUR HEALTH?

The rich aromas and therapeutic properties of herbs are mostly based on combinations of many substances. These substances can be found in different parts of the plant: the leaves, flowers, roots, bulbs, fruits, and seeds. Herbs contain, among others things, water-soluble tannins, which disinfect and cleanse mucous membranes, bitter substances that positively affect digestion, and emollient substances that soothe the skin, as well as many vitamins and minerals. However, the most important components are the essential oils that give the plants their specific aromas. Thanks to special production and preservation methods, drugs can be made from herbs.

Even though the herbs are mild and gentle, and should improve your health, you should follow suggested usages. Treat only mild ailments with herbs, since using them is no substitute for seeing your doctor.

PRESERVING AROMA AND EFFECTIVENESS

Leaves, flowers, and similar parts of the plant should be picked in the morning, as soon as they are dry. The levels of their therapeutic components will be highest after a sunny day. Leaves should be cut off prior to blooming, when they are especially tender. When cutting plants back, be careful not to over-cut them, so that they can grow back quickly. Matured seeds should be harvested in the early morning before they drop. Roots should be harvested in fall or early spring.

FRESH HERBS are especially aromatic and effective when minced. It is very important to cut them into small pieces and mash them well.

Many spices and herbs can be preserved without losing much of their aroma. There are many possibilities for storing herbs during the winter.

DRYING: shake the stems, leaves and seed heads that have been cut off to ensure that there are no insects on them. Tie into small bundles and hang upside down in a dry, airy place or lay them on screens. Put baking paper or a cotton cloth under the seed heads.

Roots should be washed and dried, then cut and hung in the same way as the stems. Large roots dry quicker if you cut them into halves or small pieces.

In humid weather, when the herbs may become moldy, you can put them in an oven or a special drying machine. Make sure that the temperature is around 95 - 105°F, because any more heat will release or destroy the essential oils. After the drying process, sift the seeds to separate them from the bracts, and store them away from bright light.

The herbal parts of the plants should be dry in 3 - 4 days; you can make sure by crushing them in your fingers. If they are still not dry, cut them into small pieces and repeat the process. Once they are dry, store them in brown bottles. Flowers and leaves will keep for about 1 year.

FREEZING: Some herbs, such as parsley, basil, thyme and chives keep their aroma best if they are thoroughly frozen in plastic bags or boxes.

VINEGAR AND OIL: Herb vinegar is easy to make. Put herbs - such as tarragon, basil, dill, or mint - into dark bottles and pour white wine vinegar over them. Let the vinegar stand from one week to several months.

To make oil infused with herbs, place a handful of herbs in some oil and let stand for 3 - 6 weeks. You can use herbs such as southernwood, marjoram, thyme, rosemary, or sage. It is important for the plants to be completely covered with oil so that they do not rot. Seal the bottles and place them on a sunny window ledge, shaking them every day. Finally, strain the oil. Refrigerating the oil in bottles enables it to keep for a long period of time. Only use high-quality vinegar and oil.

WINE AND LIQUEUR: To make white or red herb wine, place a handful of herbs in a bottle of wine, and keep it at room temperature for several weeks. To produce herb liqueur, place a handful of herbs in a bottle of brandy, and allow to stand for 3 - 4 weeks. Liqueurs should be sweetened with sugar and diluted with water. Shake before use.

HERBAL PILLOWS AND AROMATIC BAGS: Place dried herbs that contain essential oils in cotton or linen cloth. Lavender and valerian are favorites because they smell pleasant and encourage sleep.

The following advice should be helpful to you if you are unfamiliar with the encyclopedia.

The plants are arranged alphabetically according to their botanical, Latin names. The English name can be found under the botanical name. Should there be any dialect names for the herbs, you can find them in the text.

The symbols in the box give you the most important features of each individual plant at a glance. Their meanings are as follows:

Type:	*Location for growth:*	*Use:*
∞ *annual*	☼ *sunny*	✗ *cuisine*
⊙ *perennial*	◑ *partial shade*	♫ *medicinal*
	● *shade*	♈ *cosmetics*
		❀ *decoration*

Features:
❗ *Irritant, may cause allergies, may be poisonous*

Some of the plants listed may be poisonous or may evoke allergic reactions in susceptible persons. The toxicity is determined by their usage, the part of the plant used, and also by the process through which it was used. Make sure children do not eat pretty, colored flowers or fruits that may be poisonous. Follow the advice under the entry for the specific herb. Avoid using the herb if you have any doubts.

Achillea millefolium
Milfoil

Type:
∞

Location for growth:
☼ – ☀

Use:
✗ 🜨 ❀

Features:
❗

FAMILY: Composites (*Asteraceae*)

ORIGIN: Common milfoil grows naturally in temperate zones ranging from Europe to Central Asia. It is indigenous to North America, New Zealand, and Australia. It was used to curb bleeding and as a disinfectant in ancient civilizations. Its bitter components made it a useful substitute for hops in the production of beer.

FEATURES: The shrub is 12 - 30 inches tall and blooms from June to October. The blossoms are white and red and resemble umbrellas. Many of the garden types vary from yellow to carmine red. The name of the species millefolium (thousand leaves) comes from its transparent, smoothly divided leaves. The tops contain high levels of bitter substances and essential oils, which give it its characteristic aroma.

SIMILAR SPECIES: The creamy-white flowers of sweet yarrow (*Achillea ageratum*) bloom throughout the summer. When used as a spice it gives dishes a musky aroma. The smooth leaves of swamp milfoil (*A. ptarmica*) taste good with bread and butter or in salads, unlike the bitterness of *Achilea millefolium*.

LOCATION FOR GROWTH: The shrubs do not need any special treatment. They should be grown in poor, dry soil in sunny or partially shaded areas. They do not tolerate excessive wetness. As a pioneer plant, they grow quickly in fallow soil.

CULTIVATION: The plants should be planted in spring, germinated indoors or sown directly in the ground. Seedling sprouts should not be covered with soil. While blooming, leave the shrubs in place without any interference. After the harvest they quickly grow back from their roots, and when the blooming period is over the whole plant should be cut back.

HARVEST: Stems should be cut off a little above the ground, and then hung to dry. When dry, cut into pieces and store in dark boxes or bottles. To use as a spice, cut off young, fresh leaves. There are many colored species to decorate your garden with.

A SPECIAL TIP:

MILFOIL POULTICE

Milfoil poultice helps relieve stomach cramps and aids digestion. To prepare the poultice put 4 tablespoonfuls flowers and leaves into 1 quart boiling water. Let stand for 5 minutes. Dip a towel into the liquid and then wring out the towel. Put the damp towel on top of the painful place and heat with a hot-water bottle. You will see that it really works!

USE:

CUISINE:

Chopped fresh, young leaves can be spread over bread with butter or added to salads. Leaves are also delicious with cottage cheese and vegetable dishes. Heavy dishes become more digestible when the leaves are added to them.

HEALTH EFFECTS:

Milfoil contains essential oils and tannins and was used as a therapeutic plant by ancient civilizations. Tea made from the stems and flowers supports digestion and relieves cramps. It also relieves swelling, stops bleeding, and helps during menstruation. To make tea, put 2 teaspoons of the herb into 1 cup boiling water. Alcohol tinctures are used as a natural treatment for infections of the urinary tract as well as against diseases of the heart, and to help circulation. Used as a washing tincture, milfoil helps treat eczema. It also relieves sore throats when gargled.

DECORATIVE USES:

Milfoil is suitable for flowerbeds and pots, and also looks great when grown in buckets. For decorative purposes, the flowers can be placed in a vase either fresh or dried. Milfoil attracts bees.

TIP:

This herb may cause an allergic reaction in people with fair or sensitive skin; the skin will become more sensitive to sun radiation. The herb must also not be used during pregnancy.

Agastache mexicana
Mexican mint

Type:

Location for growth:
☼ – ☀

Use:
✗ ❀

FAMILY: Labiates (Labiatae)

ORIGIN: This magical herb comes from Mexico, as its name implies. Its popularity has increased thanks to its candle-like flowers and sweet aroma. The species is a favorite for growing in both flower and herb gardens, and has many attractive varieties similar to European mint.

FEATURES: This shrubby plant is 8 – 14 inches tall and is grown as an annual because of its sensitivity to low temperatures. Fleecy flower-spikes of light violet, blue, and white appear during the summer, attracting bees and butterflies. The plant's common names - such as anise-hyssop and lemon-hyssop - are derived from its aroma, which is similar to that of anise.

TIPS FOR SPECIES: "Champagne" has pink to peach-orange blossoms and smells like mint. In addition, there are varieties with a pure lemon aroma.

SIMILAR SPECIES: *Agastache foeniculum* (anise-hyssop), also known as "*A. anisata.*" It is attractive not only because of its

leaves and aroma, but also for its violet, flower-spikes which can grow 8 inches tall. It is used in sweet dishes, teas and salads, and can also be grown in some climates as a perennial.

The leaves of "*A. cana*" smell a bit like orange thyme. It is grown as a mosquito-repelling plant in its place of origin. Korean Mint (*Cedronella japonica*) was formerly classified as a member of the Agastache genus. In traditional Chinese medicine it is used to help fight colds and discomfort, and may be effective against fungal infections.

LOCATION FOR GROWTH: Sunny or partially shaded. The earth should be damp but well tilled, so that puddles do not form.

CULTIVATION: In spring it should be started in a greenhouse or on a window ledge. Young plants can be planted outdoors only after the danger of frost has passed. *Mexican mint* can be grown in groups. The ideal spacing is at least 8 inches between plants. It is important to keep the plants moist. Adding compost to the soil in spring will give the plants enough nutrients for the season.

HARVEST: The leaves should be used as fresh as possible. To avoid losing the aroma, do not over-dry.

A SPECIAL TIP:

A SUBSTITUTE FOR SUGAR
If you want to avoid using sugar, simply put some Agastache foeniculum leaves in your tea. It not only tastes good, but the substances it contains relieve the symptoms of sore throats and colds.

USE:

CUISINE:

Mexican mint can be used for tea or added to meats, sauces, soups, or salads. It tastes similar to French tarragon and is a great substitute for it. Those who do not like anise can try the varieties with mint or lemon aromas.

DECORATIVE USES:

Thanks to its big blossom spikes and valuable substances this plant is a real beauty that brings a lot of pleasure to every gardener. It also attracts butterflies, like the butterfly bush family (*Buddleja*). The plant looks great in outdoor gardens and in decorative baskets. It can also be put into a vase since its spikes stay fresh for a long time.

Allium sativum
Garlic

Type:

⊙ – ∞

Location for growth:

☼

Use:

✕ ❀

Features:

❗

FAMILY: Leek family (*Alliaceae*)

ORIGIN: Garlic originally came from central Asia, but spread all over the world thousands of years ago. It is one of the oldest therapeutic spice plants. In ancient Egypt the builders of the pyramids were given garlic to improve their stamina.

FEATURES: This plant of the onion family consists of many small bulbs, known as garlic cloves, that grow together to form a head. In summer, 40-inch stalks with white flowers arranged in round balls (umbels) appear. Garlic does not have any seeds; instead it reproduces by means of young bulbs that grow around the corolla, and which can be saved for planting next year. This plant is a perennial only in warm regions; otherwise it must be replanted every year.

TIP FOR SPECIES: There is only one species of garlic, but it can be found in many different regions. It is worth noting that garlic varieties from southern countries are not hardy enough to be grown in colder regions.

SIMILAR SPECIES: A very interesting chive variety is the garlic chive (*Allium tuberosum*), the grassy leaves of which have a subtle garlic aroma and can be used the same way as chives. It can be harvested from spring through fall and is used to garnish and flavor salads, sauces, and other dishes. Garlic chives can be dug up in the fall, separated, and grown indoors on a window ledge during the winter.

LOCATION FOR GROWTH: Garlic needs a warm, sunny place. The soil should be loose, rich in humus and nutrients, and weedless. The plant does not fare well in very wet soil.

CULTIVATION: In warmer regions the cloves should be planted during the fall and in other regions in spring. They should spaced about 4 - 6 inches apart. The ideal depth is nearly 2 inches. Plant the rows at least 8 inches apart.

HARVEST: Plants that have been planted in spring mature in the summer, while plants that are planted in fall mature the following spring. The bulbs can be harvested after the leaves become dry and bleached. Clean the bulbs, tie them together in small bundles, and hang in a dry, airy place protected against frost. They can be kept this way throughout the winter. The small cloves from the bulbs are suitable for growing but are less good for consumption.

A SPECIAL TIP:

GARLIC AND ONION SOUP
Peel 10 cloves of garlic and half a pound of onions and cut them into thin slices and add salt. Tear the leaves from a small bunch of washed marjoram. Saute half of the marjoram together with the onions and garlic. Then add 1 quart of vegetable broth and simmer for 15 minutes. Meanwhile, mix 5 tablespoons white wine with 2 teaspoons starch and add to the soup, stirring constantly. Finally add salt, pepper and the rest of the marjoram leaves, and garnish with croutons.

USE

CUISINE:
Raw or steamed garlic will add spicy flavor to salads, vegetable dishes, meat, soups and sauces. It can also be pickled in vinegar or oil.

HEALTH EFFECTS:
Besides the essential oils, garlic contains a substance known as allicin, which has a strong antibiotic effect. It disinfects and reduces blood pressure and cholesterol level, while supporting blood supply. It helps with flatulence and skin diseases. It is recommended that patients suffering from acne should rub a fresh clove of garlic on the affected area. 2 glasses of garlic milk drunk every morning on an empty stomach help alleviate stomach and intestine problems. Pound three cloves of garlic to a paste and mix this paste with 2 cups of milk to prepare garlic milk. Boil the milk briefly and strain it into a cup. However, consumption of more than 2-3 fresh cloves a day may cause stomach problems.

TIP:
Since garlic causes "skin thinning," pregnant women must not consume more than 2-3 cloves a day. When using ready-made preparations, please pay heed to the dosage information.

DECORATIVE USES:
Garlic planted amidst roses may strengthen their fragrance!

Allium schoenoprasum
Chives

Type:

Location for growth:

Use:

Features:

!

FAMILY: Leek family (*Alliaceae*)

ORIGIN: Chives come from central Europe but can also be found from the Himalayas to the Rocky Mountains. The plant is a good source of vitamins and has been used since the Middle Ages.

FEATURES: This perennial plant from the onion family consists of dark, green, thin, tubular leaves about 12 inches long, called pipes. In summer the plant produces decorative spherical flowers in light violet, dark violet or white depending on the type.

TIPS FOR SPECIES: The rough-leafed "Grolau" variety is a classic, while "Filo" produces very fine leaves. The "Alba" variety has white blooms, and "Forescate" has shiny red flowers.

SIMILAR SPECIES: In late spring bear's garlic (*Allium ursinum*) produces white umbels. The leaves of this typical forest variety contain essential oils like those found in garlic, and reduce blood pressure. Young leaves harvested before blooming can be added to salads or used in sandwiches.

After blooming, the bulbs can be dug up and used like garlic. In the garden the plant spreads profusely. The leaves of the bunching onion (*A. fistulosum*) are also tasty and nutritious.

LOCATION FOR GROWTH: A sunny or partially shaded place with soil rich in nutrients and calcium.

CULTIVATION: For an early harvest, start the seeds indoors in early winter. In May they can be planted outdoors. Older, thick plants can be divided at this point. Chives can be planted either in rows or clumps, and should be cut regularly and fertilized with compost several times. If you cut off the blossoms, the leaves will be tenderer. If you pick the leaves regularly, new leaves grow back.

HARVEST: Nearly 6 weeks after sowing, chives are ready for use. They can be harvested until fall. It is best to tear off only the thick leaves just above the earth so that they can grow back. In winter, dig the plants up and grow in pots on a window ledge. Chives are not suitable for drying, but can be frozen if necessary.

A SPECIAL TIP:

COTTAGE CHEESE-YOGURT DIP WITH CHIVES
Mix half a pound each of cottage cheese and yogurt with crushed garlic cloves, minced onion, and a bunch of chopped chives. Season the dip with salt and pepper. It is best served with fresh vegetables, meat dishes, or potatoes baked in foil.

A QUICK SOUP WITH BEAR'S GARLIC
Chop bear's garlic leaves and sauté in butter. Add vegetable bouillon and flavor with fresh cream. The soup is now ready.

USE:

CUISINE:

Chives contain a lot vitamin C, which is why they should be eaten fresh. When frozen or dried they lose most of their vitamins. This piquant plant can be used to flavor salads, cottage cheese, sandwiches, and egg dishes like omelets and scrambled eggs. They also give a nice flavor to sauces, soups, and meat dishes.

HEALTH EFFECTS:

Thanks to their high content of essential oils, chives improve digestion and also reduce blood pressure.

DECORATIVE USES:

The violet blossom umbels give the garden a pretty look. However, they appear only on leaves that have not been torn off.

AN IMPORTANT PRECAUTION:

To avoid confusing the leaves of bear's garlic with the leaves of lily-of-the-valley, which are poisonous, make sure the leaves you pick have a garlic smell, or be careful to harvest bear's garlic only in early spring before lily-of-the-valley grows. Pregnant women should keep in mind that bear's garlic, like garlic, thins the blood.

Aloysia triphylla
Lemon verbena

FAMILY: Verbena family (*Verbenaceae*)

ORIGIN: The *Aloysia* family comprises about 35 species. One of the most beautiful is Lemon verbena, also known as the lemon shrub, which is sometimes known by its older botanical name *Lippia triphylla*. It is indigenous to Uruguay, Argentina, and Chile.

FEATURES: Outdoors, the shrub grows up to 16 feet tall; grown in a pot it is usually smaller. The lancet leaves (up to 4 inches long) have a strong lemon odor if you rub them in your hand. In summer the plant produces small violet flowers in branched clusters (panicles), which also smell good.

LOCATION FOR GROWTH: Lemon verbena grows best in partial shade. A few hours of sun in the morning or evening suffice. As a rule, rich humus or potting soil is recommended when lemon verbena is grown in pots. In summer it can also be grown outdoors, but do not forget to put it in a pot and place indoors before the first frost.

CULTIVATION: During winter *Aloysia* needs a light, airy, frost-free environment, and temperatures from 35 - 40°F are just enough. If you keep it in a dark place it loses its leaves. In the winter the plant needs only enough water to keep it from drying out, but in summer the plant must be watered regularly. Before digging the plant up you can cut it back sharply and pick off the shoots. These can be rooted at a temperature of 70°F. Pinch back the young plants several times so that they can grow into small shrubs. Fertilize weekly from spring to late summer. The shrub is very vulnerable to aphids.

HARVEST: As a rule, the leaves keep best when dried and stored in sealed bottles in a dark place. The extract is known as *Herba Verbenae odoratae* and can be obtained from a pharmacy.

A SPECIAL TIP:

LIMES FROM YOUR OWN GARDEN

Lemon and lime fans can grow their own trees. They need a warmer place than lemon verbena, but can be grown in pots without much effort. If you keep them in a sunny place at temperatures ranging from 60 - 65°F during the winter they will produce delicious fruit rich in vitamin C. The juice reduces fever, has antiseptic effects, and is suitable as an ingredient in drinks and foods. It can be added to salad dressings, roasted meats, soft drinks, or cocktails. Limes are less sour than lemons, but more bitter. Lime peel is less useful, whereas ground lemon peel can be added to cakes, sauces, teas, or mulled wine.

USE:

CUISINE:
The aromatic leaves can be used in many recipes. You can add a leaf to the water, for example, to spice boiled fish. Lemon verbena leaves are also a favorite ingredient in tea in France and Spain.

HEALTH EFFECTS:
The essential oils calm down and relieve stomach cramps. Added to tea they aid digestion. Leaves added to a bath release a relaxing fragrance.

COSMETICS:
The essential oils are used in the production of perfumes and other cosmetics. You can dry the leaves yourself and use them in a potpourri.

DECORATIVE USES:
Grown in pots on your balcony or terrace they not only look nice, but smell good too! Because of their lemony aroma they should be placed near where you sit and relax.

Althaea officinalis
Marshmallow

Type:

⊙

Location for growth:

☼

Use:

✗ 🜂 🏆 ✿

FAMILY: *Malvaceae*

ORIGIN: True marshmallow originally came from central Europe but has spread to North Africa and Siberia. Earlier it was found only in wet, sultry places, but nowadays it is generally cultivated. Its health benefits were known as early as in the time of Charlemague, and its roots are used today in cough syrups.

FEATURES: The bushy, velvety marshmallow can reach a height of 6 feet. Its stalks are divided and covered with hairs. Its large, heart-shaped leaves are very decorative and are also covered with hairs. In summer the plant produces white or violet blossoms. The fleshy roots can grow as tall as 20 inches.

SIMILAR SPECIES: Hollyhock (*Alcea rosea, earlier Althaea rosea*) is used as a natural medicine like its relatives, but its blossoms are white, yellow, pink or dark red.

LOCATION FOR GROWTH: Sunny, wet places with deep soil rich in nutrients.

CULTIVATION: It is easiest to buy young plants and plant them in spring. Older and larger plants can be divided easily. Also, seeds can be collected from the plants and germinated indoors in early spring. When the young plants are strong enough they can be planted outdoors in May. Make sure the plants have enough space. In spring it is best to add some compost or organic fertilizer. If you keep the soil wet in dry weather and till it well, the marshmallow should grow well. It should be cut back before winter.

HARVEST: The roots should be dug up in the fall, cleaned, and cut into pieces. Then dry them in an oven at a temperature of 90 – 125°F until they lose the last of their moisture. Keep them in a dry, airy place. Blossoms and leaves are harvested fresh and spread on paper to dry. The leaves are best if harvested before the plant blooms.

A SPECIAL TIP:

TEA WITH MARSHMALLOW ROOTS TO ALLEVIATE COUGHING
Put 2 teaspoons chopped root into 1 cup cold water and let it sit for about 6 hours. Stir it from time to time and then strain it through linen or an especially fine strainer. Then boil the mixture and drink it in small draughts.

MARSHMALLOW TEA FOR INDIGESTION AND INTESTINAL TROUBLES
Pour 1 cup boiling water over 2 teaspoons chopped root. After 10 minutes strain the tea and drink without sugar.

USE:

CUISINE:

Thin tops of young marshmallow plants can be chopped and added to salads.

HEALTH EFFECTS:

The roots used as an ingredient in tea help against a cough and hoarseness as well as indigestion and intestinal troubles. Marshmallow tea is also calming and can be used as a gargle to relieve sore throat, mouth swelling, and irritation caused by smoking. Blossoms boiled in a little water with a lot of honey are effective against a cough.

COSMETICS:

A poultice made from marshmallow leaves heals injuries. Used as a mask it soothes the skin.

DECORATIVE USES:

Marshmallow looks traditional and pretty when placed on your front porch or against walls. The cut flowers stay fresh for a long time in a vase.

Anethum graveolens
Dill

<table>
<tr><td>

Type:

⊙

Location for growth:

Use:

</td></tr>
</table>

FAMILY: Carrot family (Apiaceae)

ORIGIN: This plant - which was used as an herb and as a remedy by the Egyptians and Romans - probably came from Asia. In the Middle Ages the Mongols brought it to Europe and since then it has spread widely.

FEATURES: Dill is easily mistaken for fennel, as it has a similar appearance and smell. It can grow up to 3 feet tall and its hollow stalks sprout smoothly feathered leaves. In late summer the plant produces many small, yellow flowers in big umbels from which the dill seeds fall. These are round and when dried they split into two pieces. A number of essential oils give the plant its distinctive aroma.

TIP FOR SPECIES: "Fern leaf dill," with leaves similar to those of ferns, is especially attractive and can be harvested for a long time.

LOCATION FOR GROWTH: Dill needs a warm, sunny place, and its smooth leaves should be protected against the wind. Grown in such a place, its aroma will be at its best. This

somewhat demanding plant requires a soil rich in nutrients, which should be well watered but not overly wet.

CULTIVATION: Dill can be sown outdoors in April, and this can be repeated every 2 or 3 weeks so that you always have the fresh herb at your disposal. Dill is especially aromatic when it blooms. If you want to harvest the plants it is recommended that you sow them in rows. If you want to let the plants mature properly, space them 8 inches from one another. Otherwise, the plants' spreading roots will keep each other from developing fully. You can grow dill among vegetables;

for example; sowing it among carrots and cucumbers is a very effective means of repelling pests. The soil should be well tilled so that puddles do not form. It is easy to start dill and in following years it will grow back.

HARVEST: The leaves can be cut off and used fresh throughout the whole year. They are especially aromatic if you cut them off after a sunny day. You can dry them or freeze them, but they tend to lose their distinctive taste. The seeds are ready to be harvested as soon as they turn brown. Cut off the seed heads and hang them upside down to dry. The mature seeds will fall out of the seed heads, so place a cloth underneath to collect them.

A SPECIAL TIP:

WINE WITH DILL TO HELP YOU FALL ASLEEP

Boil a cup of white wine and add 1 teaspoon dry seeds. Strain the wine and drink it hot. Put leaves of Greek dill plants on your eyes to help you fall asleep.

CUCUMBER YOGURT

Peel 2 small cucumbers, cut them into small pieces and mash, add 4 cloves garlic and 4 containers plain yogurt. Mix together in a bowl and garnish with a small bunch of dill and olives.

USE:

CUISINE:

Fresh leaves give a special flavor to fish, vegetable dishes, sauces, and salads. It is best to chop them before adding them to dishes. Dill is also popular for flavoring vinegars and pickles.

HEALTH EFFECTS:

Dill seed tea helps against indigestion and flatulence. It also has a calming effect, and since it is a diuretic it can be used for trouble with kidney stones. Mothers can use it to increase secretion of milk.

DECORATIVE USES:

Dill is also used in decorative gardens because of its smooth stalks and pretty yellow flower umbels. It looks especially good when planted in beds with other perennials. Its smooth stalks may also be used in bouquets.

Angelica archangelica
Angelica

FAMILY: Carrot family (*Apiaceae*)

ORIGIN: *Angelica* has spread from northern Europe into northern Asia. As a rule it grows in mountains and wet meadows. It was grown in early monastery gardens as an herb and spice. It was believed that it protected people from plague.

FEATURES: Angelica's main stalks can grow up to 6 feet tall. They are hollow and have large, markedly feathered leaves. In summer the plant produces green and white blossom umbels. Besides that, angelica roots form fleshy, deep bunches that are used as a spice or a cure. Grown in gardens, the plant often lives for 3 or 4 years.

LOCATION FOR GROWTH: Partial shade and soil rich in humus and nutrients are recommended. In such a place the plant spreads quickly.

CULTIVATION: The seeds can be germinated indoors in early spring. In spring divide the small plants and plant them 30 - 40 inches from one another. Since one plant is enough for

a home garden, it is easier to buy a young plant from your garden center. The soil should be well moistened but not extremely wet. The plant will not bear anything if kept dry. Tip: The root bunch becomes denser if you cut off the root shoots in the first year.

HARVEST: It is best to harvest the leaves before the plant flowers. You can use the flowers fresh or dried, whereas the leaves keep their best aroma after they have been dried. The roots should be dug up in fall, cleaned well, and hung to dry. They can also be dried in the oven at low temperatures. As soon as they are brittle, store them in an airy linen bag.

A SPECIAL TIP:

ANGELICA TEA

Pour a pint of hot water over 1 teaspoon dried leaves and steep for 5 minutes. Then strain and drink a cup before meals. This calms your stomach and improves your appetite.

CANDIED ANGELICA STALKS

Blanch pieces of young angelica stalks in hot water for several minutes so that the outer skin can be peeled off. Then put them in hot water again for some time, let them dry and weigh them. Boil an equal amount of sugar with a third of the amount of water until a syrup is formed, and pour it over the stalks. The next day boil the stalks again in the syrup and some water until it evaporates and the sugar crystallizes. The work of preparing this special candy is rewarding.

USE:

CUISINE:

Chopped leaves and stalks can be used to spice salads, sauces, soups, and sweet dishes. Its sweet aroma is reminiscent of anise. They can also be sautéed as vegetables. The young raw stalks are very delicious. Dried seeds and pieces of roots are popular for flavoring spirits.

HEALTH EFFECTS:

Angelica contains essential oils, bitter alkaloids, tannins and acids that support digestion. Used as a tea or tincture it relieves stomach troubles and colds.

DECORATIVE USES:

Angelica is a very pretty shrub that loses its aroma when grown in shady areas. It can be grown as a single plant or together with other plants in beds.

AN IMPORTANT PRECAUTION:

Pregnant women should avoid using angelica because it may cause abortion and damage nerves.

Anthriscus cerefolium
Chervil

Type:

∞

Location for growth:

☀

Use:

Features:

❗

FAMILY: Carrot family (*Apiaceae*)

ORIGIN: Chervil originally came from Asia and the Caucasus. It spread to the Mediterranean and from there it was brought north. Besides having aromatic leaves that can be used as a flavoring, it is popular for its blood-cleansing properties.

FEATURES: This annual grows as a shrub up to 25 inches tall. Its soft leaves are feathered and if you do not catch its sweet aroma, which is similar to that of anise, it can be easily mistaken for parsley or carrots. It contains the essential oil isoanethol in high concentrations, highest just before the plant blooms. The plant produces white blossom umbels that appear according to sowing time until late summer.

TIP FOR SPECIES: You can choose either a smooth-leaf or curly-leaf species.

SIMILAR SPECIES: Meadow chervil (*Anthriscus sylvestris*) is not suitable for use in cooking. However, the plant produces a natural yellow dye.

LOCATION FOR GROWTH: Chervil grows best in partial shade in loose, damp soil. A somewhat demanding herb, it requires few nutrients, but in dry spells it begins to bloom early, which adversely affects the taste.

CULTIVATION: This hardy plant can be sown outdoors as early as March in rows, spaced 4 – 6 inches apart. It is recommended that one sow a new row every 2 weeks, because chervil grows and blooms quickly. When sown among lettuce it repels aphids and snails. If you let some flowers mature, you can pick your own seeds for the next year. In winter, you can grow the plant on your window ledge for a good source of vitamin C. However, the germination period of 2 weeks is longer than that of cress.

HARVEST: The leaves taste best when they are young and fresh. Harvesting is possible several weeks after sowing and should be done before blooming. When frozen it keeps its aroma, however when dried and cooked for a long time it loses it.

A SPECIAL TIP:

CREAM OF CHERVIL SOUP
Pick about 4 ounces of chervil leaves. Set some aside for garnishing the soup and chop the rest. Melt 1.5 ounces butter in a pot and add about 1 ounce flour. Then add 1 cup milk and 1 pint vegetable stock and simmer for 10 minutes over low heat. Meanwhile mix the chervil with half a cup fresh cream and add it to the soup. Season with salt, pepper and a pinch of sugar. Garnish with croutons and the remaining chervil leaves.

USE:

CUISINE:

Chervil is a vital ingredient for spring soups and herb soups. Its nickname, "soup plant," was derived from this use. It is used in the classic dish Frankfurter Green Sauce, and also tastes great with fish and egg dishes, as well as with raw foods, tomatoes, and cheese. Make sure you add it to dishes just before serving; otherwise it loses its aroma.

HEALTH EFFECTS:

Essential oils and bitter substances support kidney function and digestion. It is ideal for cleansing the blood and purging your body in spring. Chervil contains a lot of vitamin C.

DECORATIVE USES:

Garden chervil is a typical garden herb. Since it is undemanding and grows well in pots, and thanks to its use as an aromatic flavoring, it should be included in every herb garden.

> **IMPORTANT PRECAUTION:**
>
> **The smooth leaves of this species may be easily confused with hemlock, which is poisonous and foul-smelling. Wild meadow chervil differs from cooking chervil in that it is slightly poisonous and may cause a skin rash.**

Apium graveolens
Celery

Type:

∞

Location for growth:

Use:

Features:

!

FAMILY: Carrot family (*Apiaceae*)

ORIGIN: The wild form of garden celery came from the Mediterranean and can now be found in most European coastal regions. There are a number of different species, such as bulb celery, stalk celery, and leaf celery. As a vegetable it contains a lot of vitamins and has a central place in the cuisines of the Greeks and Romans.

FEATURES: Unlike stalk celery, leaf celery (*Apium graveolens var. secalinum*) does not produce any bulbs, but rather thin, branched roots. Its square stalks produce dark green, sharply feathered leaves that contain essential oils and are used as a culinary herb. Since it is susceptible to frost, it is usually grown as an annual. White blossom umbels are produced, for the most part from perennial varieties.

SIMILAR SPECIES: Wild celery (*Apium graveolens* var. *dulce*) and bulb celery (*A. graveolens* var. *rapaceum*) arose from the same wild form. Both are grown in earth rich in humus and nutrients, and both require careful watering.

LOCATION FOR GROWTH: Celery requires soil that is rich in nutrients and does not dry out fast. However, it needs plenty of sun to produce its full aroma.

CULTIVATION: Celery can be harvested very early if you start the seeds indoors in early spring. The seedlings should be separated and planted outdoors in May. Leaf celery plants should be spaced 4 – 6 inches apart. The soil should be loose and without weeds. During the summer the plant requires a lot of water. Leaf celery is useful if grown next to cabbage or beans, as it repels caterpillars.

HARVEST: The leaves may be cut off at any time and used fresh as an herb. Dried or frozen leaves keep their aroma as well. The bulbs should be dug up in fall as soon as the outer leaves wilt. Stalk celery can be harvested as late as August.

A SPECIAL TIP:

SPICY HERB SALAD

For 4 portions you will need 2 ounces celery leaf, 4 ounces each chervil and watercress, a bunch each of chives and basil, 2 bunches of smooth parsley, and 1 – 2 bunches of cress. Wash and dry all of the herbs except for the cress. Cut the leaves from the stalks, chop the chives finely, and chop the cress. To prepare the dressing mince 4 ounces red onion, add 2 tablespoonfuls wine vinegar and 3 tablespoonfuls oil and season with salt, fresh ground pepper and a pinch of sugar. Mix all the herbs together, add the vinaigrette and the salad is ready.

USE:

IMPORTANT PRECAUTION:
Celery juice and tea have strong diuretic effects. People who suffer from kidney diseases should consult their doctors before using celery.

CUISINE:
Fresh or dried, the leaves are used for seasoning sauces, salads, stews, and soups. Like its bulbs, the leaves are great in soups. Stalk celery can be served with a dip or in salads. The bulbs taste good fresh or stewed.

Bulb celery

HEALTH EFFECTS:

The leaves contain an essential oil that has strong diuretic and blood cleansing effects. Stalk celery and bulb celery fight rheumatism.

Armoracia rusticana
Horseradish

Type:
☉

Location for growth:
☼ – ☀

Use:
✕ 🜊 ✿

Features:
❗

FAMILY: Mustard family (*Brassicaceae*)

ORIGIN: Horseradish was originally found in an area reaching from southeast Europe to west Asia. In the 12th century it spread to northern and central Europe. It was very popular at that time, and was used as a preparation against intestinal worms.

FEATURES: This perennial produces bright rosettes of slightly corrugated leaves that may grow up to 3 feet long. The following year, in late summer, the plant produces blooming shoots up to 5 feet long with white aromatic flowers in loose clusters. However, of most interest are the thick, fleshy, brown roots, which are white inside. They contain a lot of vitamin C and a potent essential oil (mustard oil glucoside) containing sulfur, which give the characteristic sharp horseradish taste. In some dialects, horseradish is known as folk's mustard or sore cleaner.

LOCATION FOR GROWTH: Horseradish grows well in the sun as well as in partial shade. The soil should be deep and rich in nutrients, and moist enough for the plant to grow large

roots. Besides that, the plant requires lots of space and should be grown in the same place for several years.

CULTIVATION: The side roots, or shoots which grow off the main root and are about 8 inches long, are easily propagated. You can cut them off from the main root at harvest time, obtain them at your garden center or order them through the post. In spring or fall plant them extended in the soil, spaced 16 inches apart, and make sure the upper end is covered with half an inch of earth. Before doing so, remove all the side roots and projections - repeat this once again in summer so that the plants lie free and then cover them again with earth. Good watering is as important as loose soil. Precaution: Horseradish spreads very quickly, so it should be grown with care.

HARVEST: The roots may be harvested throughout the year, provided the ground is not frozen. In winter you can keep horseradish in a cold place covered with wet sand. It may be used fresh or dried, and when cut into pieces or ground, it can be also frozen.

A SPECIAL TIP:

THIS POULTICE ALLEVIATES HEADACHES. **Mix half a teaspoonful ground horseradish root with 2 – 3 tablespoonfuls water and wrap in linen. Place the linen on the nape of your neck. Check to make sure that your neck does not turn red.**

FOR GOOD DIGESTION
Before going to bed drink 1 cup warm milk with about 1 cc fresh ground horseradish root.

USE:

CUISINE:

Fresh ground roots add a sharp flavor to meat and egg dishes, but horseradish should be used with care. It is especially popular when used with beef or smoked salmon. Pieces of the roots are used as an ingredient for pickling gherkins.

HEATH EFFECTS:

Horseradish supports digestion and has diuretic and antibiotic effects. Applications of ground horseradish relieve such diseases as rheumatism, arthritis, and ischemia.

DECORATIVE USES:

Due to its size, horseradish is not suitable for smaller herb gardens. Once it is grown, it is difficult to get rid of. However, if you do not wish to do without it you can grow horseradish in pots without any special effort.

IMPORTANT PRECAUTION:

Sharp horseradish can irritate skin and mucous membranes. It can cause some people's skin to turn red or to take on the appearance of a suntan. When used as a food it can irritate the stomach, intestines, or kidneys. Pregnant women and nursing mothers should therefore avoid using it.

Arnica montana
Arnica

FAMILY: Daisy family (*Asteraceae*)

ORIGIN: True arnica or mountain tobacco is indigenous to European mountains but can also be found in peat and heather bogs. It has been known as an herb for centuries. As is true of its wild predecessors, only from time to time has arnica been cultivated. In France it is known as "Alpine tobacco," since its powdered leaves have been used for snuff.

FEATURES: An erect shrub with long leaves and a resinous aroma, it can grow up to 20 inches tall. Its large, light yellow flowers appear on simple stalks and have the same smell. They are produced, according to the weather, from June to August, sometimes until early fall. Besides essential oils, arnica also contains flavine, alkaloids and tannins.

SIMILAR SPECIES: *Arnica chamissonis* originally came from North America. It contains the same useful substances as its related species and can be grown in any garden soil.

LOCATION FOR GROWTH: The plant prefers full sun but also grows quite well in partial shade. It requires acidic

soil rich in nutrients, which its natural environment affords.

CULTIVATION: In early spring arnica can be germinated indoors. The seeds should be as fresh as possible. Make sure you plant the seeds in soil rich in nutrients and with a low pH. In late summer plant the young plants outdoors, where they will bloom in one year. You can also propagate the plants from root rhizomes. As *Arnica montana* grows well only in acidic soil, it may be necessary to spread the ground with soil that is used for rhododendrons and with soft rainwater. *Arnica chamissonis* is not terribly demanding and adding compost or fertilizer in the spring is sufficient. In hot summers the plants should be watered, and in winter they should be mulched to protect against frost.

HARVEST: The heads of the flowers should be cut off on a sunny day and hung in a shaded place to dry. You can also dry them in the oven but the temperature should not be higher than 100°F. The roots should be dug up in September and hung the same way for drying.

A SPECIAL TIP:

SOOTHING MASSAGE OIL
Warm 4 tablespoonfuls olive oil and pour it over 1 tablespoonful dried arnica flowers, then leave in a dark place for about 30 minutes. Stir the liquid from time to time and finally strain. The oil should be kept in dark bottles in the refrigerataor.

ARNICA TEA FOR TONSILLITIS
Pour a cup of boiling water over 1 – 2 tablespoonfuls fresh or dried flowers, then strain after 10 minutes. The tea should be gargled several times a day in small draughts. You can also make a compress from the tea to heal wounds and sprained joints.

USE:

HEALTH EFFECTS:

Arnica helps repair damage to the body by relieving swelling and improving blood circulation. Arnica ointment or compresses relieve the pain of bruises, contusions, and sprained joints. The tincture relieves headaches and rheumatism. If you put 1 – 2 tablespoonfuls of the tincture into a glass of lukewarm water you get a gargle that relieves swelling. Precaution: Since the tincture is poisonous, spit it out after gargling.

COSMETICS:

A tincture of arnica cleanses dirty skin quickly.

DECORATIVE USES:

The yellow flowers are very beautiful in gardens or pots. They look especially lovely when placed in front of dark tree species. In a vase they will stay fresh for a long time.

IMPORTANT PRECAUTION:

If you use arnica on yourself be very careful and use it only externally. The plant contains a poison, and overdoses can cause heart problems.

Artemisia abrotanum
Southernwood

Type:
⊙

Location for growth:
☼

Use:
✕ 🜨 ⚱ ❀

Features:
❗

FAMILY: Daisy family (*Asteraceae*)

ORIGIN: Monks brought southernwood from western Asia to Europe about 1,000 years ago. Thanks to its therapeutic properties it was grown in monastery and private gardens for centuries. It was considered to have considerable magical capabilities, protecting people from plague and stimulating hair growth.

FEATURES: The aromatic shrubs produce finely feathered gray-green leaves, which give off a pleasant lemony aroma. They grow about 25 – 40 inches tall and produce pure white blossom heads until fall. Essential oils, alkaloids, and tannins give them a bitter taste.

SIMILAR SPECIES: Southernwood is a relative of wormwood (*Artemisia absinthium*). A tea made of wormwood leaves helps with indigestion and intestinal troubles and also relieves pain during menstruation. It is also useful for influenza and colds. The 'Powis Castle' and 'Lambrook Silver' species produce silvery, glistening leaves and are not hard to grow in shrub gardens. Mugwort (*A. vulgaris*) has the same

characteristics. The dried leaves are an important ingredient in Chinese medicine.

LOCATION FOR GROWTH: The full aroma is produced if the plant is grown in a sunny, warm place. Well-drained, sandy soil with lime is ideal.

CULTIVATION: Southernwood is not grown from seed, so it is necessary to obtain small plants at your garden center in spring or summer. You can also ask your neighbors or relatives if they have a shrub from which you can cut some rhizomes. If you regularly cut off the rhizomes the plant remains shrubby and does not grow too high. Woody stalks can be cut with ease in spring. Protection is necessary only during very cold winters.

HARVEST: Thin tops of the shoots can be cut off throughout the summer. For drying, cut off the branches whole in late summer.

A SPECIAL TIP:

MOTH REPELLENT

The intensive aroma of southernwood repels pests. If you place some dried branches in your wardrobe they should repel moths. The aromatic leaves spread over vegetable beds repel caterpillars. Even some birds have learned about these effects and therefore use southernwood branches for their nests.

WORMWOOD TEA

Pour 1 cup boiling water over 1–2 spoonfuls wormwood and steep for 10 minutes. After meals drink without sugar. If you find it too bitter use half of the amount of wormwood and add peppermint leaves.

USE:

CUISINE:
Southernwood can be used as a spice for sauces, salads, and roasts. Use sparingly, because it is highly aromatic.

HEALTH EFFECTS:
This herb supports appetite and helps with stomach troubles and indigestion. Its essential oils have disinfecting properties and therefore southernwood and wormwood have been used against worms. The tea helps during menstruation.

COSMETICS:
The essential oils are important ingredients of perfumes. Its branches may also be used for potpourri. If you have oily skin, add some branches to your bath water.

DECORATIVE USES:
This smooth, gray-green plant looks wonderful, but not only as a part of flowerbeds. The shoots can be used for floral or aromatic bouquets.

IMPORTANT PRECAUTION:

If you use wormwood for a long period of time its substances can damage your nervous system. Since southernwood and wormwood intensify bleeding, pregnant women should avoid their use.

Artemisia dracunculus
Tarragon

Type:
⊙

Location for growth:
☀ – ☀

Use:
✕ 𝕬

FAMILY: Daisy family (*Asteraceae*)

ORIGIN: Its original home was in the steppes of southern Russia and Mongolia, but over the years, it spread to the Mediterranean. In German-speaking countries it is known as "Schlangenkraut" (snake shrub), while the French call it "herbe de dragon" (dragon plant), as it was believed to heal snakebites.

FEATURES: The shrubby plant has slender stalks which produce long, thin leaves. There are two predecessors: one is the robust, bitter Russian tarragon, which grows up to 5 feet tall, and the other is aromatic French tarragon, which has a sweet taste reminiscent of anise seed and grows to about 8 – 12 inches tall. Unlike Russian tarragon, French tarragon does not bloom in northern regions, but when either type of tarragon does flower, it produces small, yellow-green heads of flowers in loose panicles from summer to fall. French tarragon is especially well known because it contains many essential oils, tannins, and bitter alkaloids.

LOCATION FOR GROWTH: the plant grows best in warm, sunny places, but also grows well in partial shade. As a somewhat demanding plant it requires soil rich in humus and nutrients, and it should be watered well. However, the plant cannot tolerate an extremely wet environment.

CULTIVATION: French tarragon can be propagated only by dividing the roots. As one or two plants are enough for domestic use, it is recommended that you obtain young plants at your garden center and space them 10 - 15 inches apart. Tarragon requires a lot of space and grows happily next to lovage. In dry summers it must be well watered, and in fall it can be cut back. In 3 – 4 years tarragon reaches its maturity and new plants should be grown. French tarragon is susceptible to frost and must be covered in winter, while Russian tarragon survives well at lower temperatures. In summer, Russian tarragon can be sown directly outdoors and later thinned.

HARVEST: The young tops of the shoots and leaves can be harvested throughout the summer. They should be used fresh because after drying they loose much of their aroma. On the other hand, frozen tarragon keeps its full flavor.

A SPECIAL TIP:

BÉARNAISE SAUCE
Mince two shallots and tear off the leaves from a bunch of tarragon. Put in a pot with half a cup of white wine and boil until about 3 tablespoonfuls are left. Strain the mixture and put into a smaller pot which has been placed in a hot water bath. Now add 3 egg yolks and stir. Next add 5 ounces butter cut into small pieces. Finally, season with salt and pepper. The water bath should NOT boil, or else the sauce will curdle.

TARRAGON VINEGAR
Place a branch of tarragon in a bottle of white wine vinegar for 2 - 3 weeks. If you like, add lemon or dill.

USE:

CUISINE:

For cooking, aromatic French tarragon is most widely used. It has a very intense flavor, so it should be used with care. It is usually added to salads, soups, and sauces or used as a spice for poultry or fish. It can be also be used for preparing herbal oils and vinegars, and to flavor tarragon mustard - and it is also used for pickling gherkins!

HEALTH EFFECTS:

Tarragon is widely known to aid digestion, and it also has diuretic effects. In the past it was used as a cure for worms.

Barbarea vulgaris
Winter Cress

Type:

Location for growth:

Use:

FAMILY: Mustard family (*Brassicaceae*)

ORIGIN: Winter cress (also known as Common Garden Yellow Rocket) originally came from Europe. However, it has spread widely and now grows from Turkey through the Caucasus and on to China, as well as in South Africa, North America and Australia. The plant is dedicated to St. Barbara, a patron of mountain people, stone quarry workers and lightning.

FEATURES: Like all biennials, winter cress produces leaves in the first year and yellow flowers the next spring. It grows from 12 to 25 inches high. The leaves contain a lot of vitamin C and have a sharp taste, similar to watercress or arugula.

TIP FOR SPECIES: The "Variegata" species is best suited for partially shaded places in gardens. Its pretty flowers are yellow and it readily reseeds itself.

LOCATION FOR GROWTH: Winter cress grows best in partial shade and wet, loose soil.

CULTIVATION: It can be sown in spring and fall. Once sown it propagates itself.

HARVEST: Fresh leaves can be harvested until winter, and its vitamin content gives you energy in cold seasons.

A SPECIAL TIP:

HERB SALAD WITH VITAMINS

Wash and dry 1 head of lettuce, 1 head of romaine lettuce, a bunch of winter cress, a bunch each of watercress, chives, parsley, basil, and mint, and a bunch of garden cress. Chop the chives, parsley, and cresses, and cut the leaves of basil and mint from their stalks. Cut oranges into halves. Rub the salad bowl with cut garlic cloves, add the herbs and mix well. To prepare a dressing mix 2 tablespoonfuls olive oil, 2 tablespoonfuls wine vinegar, 1 tablespoonful lemon juice, 2 crushed cloves of garlic, 1 tablespoonful brown sugar and 1 tablespoonful tarragon mustard.

USE

CUISINE:

Because of its high vitamin content, winter cress should be at your disposal especially in winter. It gives a sharp, spicy taste to fish. Smart people take care of their winter supply of vitamins in advance, and some herbs can be harvested in winter or stay green under the snow. In addition to winter cress, these are: common scurvy-grass, parsley, anise, miner's lettuce and sorrel. Covering them with spruce branches protects them in the winter.

HEALTH EFFECTS:

Winter cress supports the appetite, cleanses the blood, and also has diuretic effects. The leaves can be used for a natural poultice.

DECORATIVE USES:

The yellow flowers are really beautiful in summer herb gardens and they attract bees. Winter cress looks especially wonderful when grown in the front parts of beds and in narrow beds.

Borago officinalis
Borage

FAMILY: Borage family (Boraginaceae)

ORIGIN: Borage spread throughout the entire Mediterranean area after the Arabs began growing it in Spain. From Spain, it spread to northern Europe, where it was known as a healing plant and culinary herb.

FEATURES: This shrubby annual plant with strong stalks and bristles can grow up to 30 inches tall. The long, oval leaves are also covered with bristles and have a strong cucumber aroma. The light blue flowers, typically star-shaped, bloom the whole summer. They can be eaten, as can the leaves, and contain a lot of vitamins, minerals and tannins, as well as essential oils.

TIP FOR SPECIES: The 'Alba' species' has white blooms, while 'Variegata' has blue ones. The latter has decorative, whitish-yellow, spotted leaves.

LOCATION FOR GROWTH: Borage can be grown in a sunny or partially shaded place. Soil rich in nutrients and calcium is very important. The soil should also be loose because of the plant's long roots.

CULTIVATION: In late spring, the plant can be sown directly in beds. Sow plenty of the large seeds, cover with soil and use only the strongest young plants. As borage quickly produces small plants, spacing is very important. The plant wilts quickly and therefore needs a lot of water. Other than that it does not require any special care. If you let some flowers mature, it can easily reseed itself.

Harvest: Young, smooth leaves can be harvested throughout the summer. They should be used fresh, not cooked. They can be frozen but when dried they lose a lot of their aroma. The pretty blue flowers can also be used fresh. You can dry and store them in closed bottles to use during the winter.

A special tip:

Salad dressing

Wash 3 fresh borage leaves, some tarragon, and a bunch of dill. Chop into small pieces and add some lemon pulp. Peel and mince a small onion. Mix half a cup of buttermilk with 2 table-spoonfuls sour cream and add the herbs and onion. Season with salt, pepper and nutmeg. The dressing can be used for cucumber or potato salad, or even better as a dip for raw vegetables.

Mask for dry skin

Cover a spoonful of borage leaves with a half-cup of water, and allow to sit until the tea is lukewarm. Then strain the mixture through a paper filter and mix with 1 egg yolk, 1 spoonful almond oil and 7 portions of fresh yeast. The mask can be used on the face, hands and breasts. Leave on for 15 minutes.

USE:

CUISINE:

Chopped borage leaves are used to season cottage cheese, soups, fish, and dishes with eggs, and they are an important ingredient in the classic dish Frankfurter Green Sauce. They taste especially good in cucumber salads. They are used fresh and added to dishes just before serving. The flowers, which can also be eaten, are used to garnish dishes and drinks.

HEALTH EFFECTS:

Borage tea cleanses the blood and also has diuretic effects. Its juice relieves coughs and bronchitis, and is believed to be good for rheumatism, as well as heart and kidney diseases. In the past, borage was believed to elevate one's mood. That is why it is also known as the "plant of good cheer."

COSMETICS:

Compounds in borage support blood circulation to the skin.

DECORATIVE USES:

Thanks to its interesting form and blue flowers, borage is a very decorative plant. It grows nicely in vegetable plots as well as in flower gardens. Its flowers attract bees, thanks to its nectar.

Calendula officinalis
Marigold

Type:

∞

Location for growth:

Use:

FAMILY: Mustard family (*Asteraceae*)

ORIGIN: Marigolds are indigenous to southern Europe and Asia. In central Europe the marigold has consistently been present in country gardens over the centuries, thanks to its use in the treatment of injuries.

FEATURES: This annual has stalks and leaves covered with soft hairs. It flowers throughout the summer; the blossoms are light yellow to dark orange. Meanwhile new species have been developed, such as brown and full-blossomed marigolds. Marigolds contain many essential oils, alkaloids, saponin, and pigments.

TIP FOR SPECIES: The 'Gitana' series are suitable for growing in beds, strip beds, and balcony pots, thanks to their modest height. The blossoms of the 'Kablouna' type are full, and the plant grows to about 20 inches in height. The 'Pacific' mixture is interesting because of its pretty flowers, which are suitable for cutting.

LOCATION FOR GROWTH: Marigolds can be grown in any garden, in full sun or half-shade.

CULTIVATION: The seeds should be sown directly in beds during March, spaced 8 – 12 inches apart. If the climate is mild it is also possible to do this in the fall. In the following years the plant reseeds itself. If you want to avoid that, decapitate regularly. If you do this, the plant blooms more and more, and in doing so you can extend the blooming period. Make sure the growth is not too thick; otherwise the plants may be attacked by fungi or aphids.

Harvest: The flowers can be picked from summer to fall. It is best to harvest them after a sunny day. They can be used fresh or dried. To dry them, carefully lay them next to each other on paper. Tender young leaves can be also used for preparing tea.

A special tip:

Marigold hand cream.
Boil 1 handful dried flowers in half a cup of olive oil and let sit for 20 minutes. Strain the mixture through a filter while pressing the flowers. Add 3 drops lemon balm oil and half an ounce of beeswax, and mix well. Fill bottles with the cream. With use several times a day your hands and cuticles will become especially soft.

Marigold oil
Put dried flowers into a dark bottle and fill with olive oil or sunflower oil. It can be stored in a cold, dark place for a long time.

USE:

CUISINE:

The flowers can be used to garnish salads and soups, adding a piquant flavor. You can try adding them to omelets or rice. In the past the flowers were used to color butter, cheese, soups, and rice dishes.

HEALTH EFFECTS:

Marigold compresses can be used for injuries, boils, or sunburn. Tea from the flowers and leaves relieves stomachaches and intestinal ailments. It may also be used as a gargle or for rinsing irritations in the mouth and pharynx. Drinking relieves menstrual problems. Lately a biological solvent has been produced from marigold, which does not damage health.

COSMETICS:

Marigold compresses soothe raw and swollen skin. In the past women would dye their hair with marigold.

DECORATIVE USES:

Marigold is a popular plant for gardens due to its pretty, bright blossoms. It quickly fills empty places with its fast growth, and can also be grown in vegetable gardens. In a vase the flowers stay fresh for about 2 weeks.

Carum carvi
Caraway

Type:
☉ – ∞

Location for growth:
☼

Use:
✕ 🐜 ✿

Features:
❗

FAMILY: Daisy family (*Apiaceae*)

ORIGIN: Caraway came from Mediterranean Europe and then spread to central Asia. It usually grows in wet meadows. As early as the time of ancient Rome it was used and considered a valuable spice. In the Middle Ages people used to wear small bags of its seeds around their necks because they believed it protected them from witches.

FEATURES: This biennial plant produces leaf rosettes in the first year, from which a stalk with blossoms grows only in the second year. It can grow up to 3 feet tall. The double seeds fall from large umbels of white flowers. When the seeds are mature they split into two single seeds. They contain tannins, essential oils and nutritious oils.

SPECIES: Besides biennial caraway, there is also a type which can be sown in spring and harvested in late summer of the same year.

SIMILAR SPECIES: "Love-in-a-mist" (*Nigella damascena*), a relative of black caraway from the Ranunculaceae family, is

mostly known as a summer flower. Its seeds, whether ground or not, have the intense flavor of woodruff.

LOCATION FOR GROWTH: Caraway requires a sunny, warm place. As it produces deep roots it needs deep, moist soil. However, it does not like excessive watering.

CULTIVATION: It should be sown with 12 inch spacing in April. The shoots should not be covered with earth. The soil should be loose and most. In cold winters, cover the plants with brushwood.

HARVEST: In the first year the young leaves can be used to flavor soups and salads. The seeds are harvested the following year just before they mature. As soon as the heads turn brown, cut them off and hang them in a dry and shaded place.

A SPECIAL TIP:

KAMMIN

Crush 2 ounces caraway seeds in a mortar and put into a bottle of pure brandy. Allow to sit for 10 days and then strain. A shot of kammin after a rich meal does wonders.

POTATOES WITH CARAWAY

Potatoes taste especially good if you put salt and caraway into the water while the potatoes are boiling. Alternatively, they can be served with herbal cottage cheese after they are sprinkled with caraway and baked on a cookie sheet.

PIQUANT CABBAGE

Add 4 – 6 tablespoonfuls oil and 1 – 2 tablespoonfuls fruit vinegar to a pound of cabbage cut into pieces. Mix well and add salt, pepper, 1 spoonful caraway and crushed garlic.

USE:

IMPORTANT PRECAUTION:
When used regularly the essential oils in caraway may cause stomach and intestinal troubles. That is why the daily recommended maximum dose of caraway is one-fifth of an ounce, or 3 – 6 drops of caraway oil with each dish.

CUISINE:
The spicy caraway is especially suitable for homemade dishes, making them easily digestible. After a shot of caraway-infused brandy, such as aquavit, food does not stay in the stomach as long. Caraway seeds are used with roasts, goulash, cabbage, sauerkraut, potatoes, soups, and salads. Sprinkling caraway over bread before baking makes it very tasty.

HEALTH EFFECTS:
Caraway calms your stomach and encourages the appetite. It also helps against stomach cramps and flatulence. To prepare a soothing tea put a spoonful of caraway seeds into a cup of boiling water.

DECORATIVE USES:

If the plant is grown in a bed it produces strong shrubs and promises a great harvest of caraway seeds. Besides that, it is a decorative plant thanks to its many red blossom umbels.

Cochlearia officinalis
Common scurvy-grass

FAMILY: Mustard family (*Brassicaceae*)

ORIGIN: Common scurvy-grass is indigenous to northern Europe, where it grows especially in coastal regions in wet, salty soil. The plant contains a lot of vitamins, is pickled in salt, and seamen used it on their long journeys as protection against scurvy, hence its name.

FEATURES: Common scurvy-grass is a shrub that produces rosettes of leaves, and grows mostly as a biennial. The plant is about 12 inches tall and has long, spoon-shaped, shafted leaves which stay green in frost. In summer the plant produces white honey-scented blossoms in thick umbels. The taste of the leaves is reminiscent of parsley, which is why it is also called "love parsley." It contains a lot of vitamin C, minerals, tannins and alkaloids, as well as mustard glucoside and a sulfur-containing essential oil.

LOCATION FOR GROWTH: Common scurvy-grass can be grown in any soil that has the proper amount of moisture and either full or half sun. It grows especially well in places that are wet and cool in summer. The plant does not tolerate much midday sun.

CULTIVATION: You can sow this plant in spring or late summer, either starting seeds indoors or sowing them directly outdoors. It is best to sow the seeds in rows and later thin to a distance of 4 inches. It is very important to water the baby plants regularly and keep the earth tidy and loose. Once the plant has been sown, it reseeds itself the following year. If you cover the plant with spruce branches in the winter, you can harvest its green leaves throughout the winter.

HARVEST: The leaves can be harvested all year long. They should be used fresh because you can also benefit from the nutritious juice from its stalks and leaves.

A SPECIAL TIP:

WILD HERB SALAD
Wash and chop 1 small purslane, 2 ounces each common scurvy-grass, common sorrel and dandelion, 4 to-matoes and 2 onions. For dressing, mix 2 containers of low fat yogurt, half a cup fruit vinegar, 2 teaspoonfuls mustard, 2 – 3 tablespoonfuls ketchup, 2 – 3 tablespoonfuls quince jelly and 1 tablespoonful curry powder. Blend until smooth. Flavor with some lemon juice, salt, pepper, sugar, and cayenne pepper.

USE:

CUISINE:
Fresh leaves containing a lot of vitamins can be added to salads. They also taste good with potatoes or cottage cheese and can easily be spread on bread. If you do not like the sharp taste of the leaves or juice, mix with other greens.

HEALTH EFFECTS:
Common scurvy-grass fights germs and strengthens the metabolism. It also supports the gall-bladder and liver and has mild secretory effects. Thanks to its body-cleansing properties, it can be used as a blood-cleansing cure in spring. If used regularly in foods, it also relieves rheumatism.

DECORATIVE USES:
The pretty shape of its leaves and its sweet-smelling blossoms make this plant decorative outside the vegetable garden. They can also be grown on your balcony in pots. Aside from that, its blossoms, which are full of nectar, attract bees and butterflies. It is also suitable for vases.

Coriandrum sativum
Coriander

Type:
∞

Location for growth:
☼

Use:

FAMILY: Carrot family (*Apiaceae*)

Origin: This plant originally came from the Middle East, but has spread from the Mediterranean to Central Europe. In the Middle Ages, it was used to repel fleas and lice.

FEATURES: This annual produces branched shoots up to 30 inches tall. The lower leaves are rounded and less feathered than the upper, younger leaves. The leaves have a very powerful smell reminiscent of bedbugs, so it is tricky to use in cooking. Its alternative names – "bedbug plant" or "bedbug dill" – derive from its smell. In summer, the plant produces white or red flower umbels. Spicy seeds grow from the flowers.

TIP FOR SPECIES: The small seeds of coriander have a nutty aroma and contain many essential oils. Leaf coriander (*Cilantro*) is used like parsley. Fresh leaves are vital in Indian curry dishes as well as Mexican, Arab and Chinese cuisine.

LOCATION FOR GROWTH: Coriander grows well only in sunny, warm places. The earth should be loose and rich in calcium.

CULTIVATION: From April to May the seeds may be sown about half an inch deep in the earth, about 12 inches apart. To avoid the work of thinning, sow in rows spaced 6 inches apart. Repeated sowing is recommended so that you have a fresh harvest all the time. Make sure the soil stays loose and hoe it from time to time. Other than that, the plant does not need any special care.

HARVEST: The seeds should be harvested before they fall out, which is when they turn brown. Cut off the seed heads and hang them up to dry. The dried seeds can be stored in closed bags. Crush the seeds just before cooking so that the aroma stays fresh.

A SPECIAL TIP:

AFELIA: CYPRIOT PORK RAGOUT

Mix 4 tablespoonfuls ground seeds in a bowl with a teaspoonful each sugar, salt and pepper. Sprinkle the mixture over 1 pound pork cutlets and marinade for 3 hours. Next, heat 3 tablespoonfuls of olive oil in a pan and brown the meat quickly. Meanwhile heat the oven to 600°F and put the meat in a pan. Now sauté 2 chopped onions in the leftover oil, add 10 ounces red wine, salt and black pepper, and let boil for a few minutes. Pour over the meat and bake for one hour. When finished, garnish the meat with fresh coriander leaves.

USE:

CUISINE:
Coriander is used in cabbage dishes, sauerkraut or salads, and as a spice for soups, meat, and fish. The spice is a classic ingredient in gingerbread and in India it is an important ingredient in curry powder. The seeds are used for stews and the production of liqueurs.

HEALTH EFFECTS:
Mild stomach and intestinal problems, such as flatulence, can be effectively treated with coriander. To make tea, put 1 – 2 tablespoonfuls of the seeds into a cup of hot water and steep for 10 minutes. Coriander can be mixed with caraway or cardamom in a tea mixture.

DECORATIVE USES:
The pretty blossom umbels look great in beds as well as in bouquets. However, not everybody likes the plant's herbal aroma.

Crocus sativus
Saffron

Type:
☉

Location for growth:
☼

Use:
✗ 🜂 ❀

Features:
❗

FAMILY: Iris family (*Iridaceae*)

ORIGIN: Saffron has always been the most expensive spice in the world. It originated in the Orient and was brought to Spain by the Moors, and can still be found in these cultures. In Europe saffron is grown in Spain and Greece, but fields of saffron can be also seen from Iran to China. Its high price is due to the fact that for 2 pounds of spice at least 100,000 stigmas must be harvested. Saffron yellow was considered a symbol of light, and so rulers' clothes were dyed with it.

FEATURES: This 3 inch tall plant grows from corms and belongs to the crocus genus. From September to November the plant produces violet-blue blossoms with long, red ovaries. The leaves, which are reminiscent of blades of grass, are produced at the same time. The red stigmas contain essential oils, bitter substances, and yellow dye (crocein).

SIMILAR SPECIES: Saffron belongs to the same species as the popular garden crocuses that bloom in spring.

LOCATION FOR GROWTH: A warm, sunny place is very important. The earth should contain humus and be well tilled.

CULTIVATION: You can choose either young plants or corms. As saffron survives only in warm regions it is advisable to dig up the corms in fall and plant them in pots. Make sure that you plant them deep enough for the tops to be barely visible. A pot with a diameter of 10 inches is suitable for 6 corms. The corms should not rot, so mix the soil with sand and make sure that water can easily drain from it. Store the pots in a cold but frost-free place. In the first year, leaves are produced which will wilt in the summer. At this time the plants should be left to dry. In September, the plants start blooming after being watered well. Later new corms form, and these can be harvested. The corms should be covered with brushwood or compost to protect them from frost. It is recommended that new plants be grown every 3 – 5 years.

HARVEST: The thrice-separated reddish stigmas should be dried after the harvest and stored in closed boxes. Before use, crush the saffron fibers in a mortar into powder. Bulbs as well as saffron powder can be purchased in supermarkets.

A SPECIAL TIP:

SAFFRON SAUCE

The basic ingredient is béchamel sauce. To prepare it, put 2 – 3 tablespoonfuls flour in a dry warm pan and cook for a short time. Do not let the flour brown. After it cools down, add 1 quart milk, a bay leaf and 1 tablespoon vegetable bouillon. Bring to a boil. Chop 1 onion, sauté and add it to the béchamel sauce with salt, pepper and nutmeg. Then add 4 – 5 teaspoons ground mustard seeds and cook together. Finally, season the sauce with half a teaspoon saffron and either cognac, sherry or port.

USE:

CUISINE:
Saffron is used to spice fish soups and rice dishes such as paella, also giving them an attractive color. It also makes sauces and bread tastier, but it should be used with care because of its bitter taste.

HEALTH EFFECTS:
The spice strengthens the heart and helps with anemia and exhaustion. It is also considered an aphrodisiac, especially in the Orient. In homeopathy it is used for helping people relax and against depression.

DECORATIVE USES:
Saffron is very pretty as a garden crocus when grown in beds or pots. It blooms in late fall.

IMPORTANT PRECAUTION:
Saffron is a component in many natural medicines, strengthening the uterus and relieving menstrual cramps. But if you exceed the recommended dose it may cause miscarriage.

Cymbopogon flexuosus
Lemongrass

Type:

∞

Location for
growth:

☼ – ☀

Use:

FAMILY: *Poaceae*

ORIGIN: Lemongrass, known in East-Asian cuisine as "Sereh," originally came from India and was brought to tropical Africa and Central America by immigrants.

FEATURES: It grows rapidly in its home and can be up to 6 feet tall. The green stalks resemble grass, and are white and fleshy in the lower third of the plant. They contain a lot of essential oil (citronella). In northern countries the plant is often grown in pots.

SIMILAR SPECIES: *Cymbopogon citratus* has its origin in the Malaysian Archipelago but is similar only in terms of its appearance and use. In special shops you can also get plants with a different taste, such as Citronella (*C. nardus*), which is much sweeter. The leaves of palmarosa grass (*C. martinii*) smell a lot like roses. The essential oil is used in the production of cosmetics and perfumes.

LOCATION FOR GROWTH: Lemongrass can be grown in full sun or partial shade. It requires earth rich in nutrients and should always be wet.

CULTIVATION: This grass requires a warm environment and is, as a rule, best kept as a houseplant. In the summer it can be placed outdoors, but it is not frost resistant. Besides good light, regular watering and fertilizing are also very important. After winter, cut the stalks as low as possible. Large shrubs may be divided.

HARVEST: Lemongrass can be harvested continuously and added fresh to dishes. It can also be dried or frozen. The white, fleshy part of the stalks can be ground into a powder or cream and is sold in shops.

A SPECIAL TIP:

EXOTIC SHRIMP SAUCE

Mash 1 medium-sized tomato, 1 teaspoon cumin, 3 red hot chili peppers, 1 piece ginger (about 1 inch), 5 shallots, and 3 cloves of garlic together with a stalk of lemongrass which has been cut into small pieces and roasted in a little oil in advance. Put half a pound of shrimp into the sauce. Then add half a cup of fish bouillon and season with salt and pepper. This sauce goes especially well with roasted or fried fish.

USE:

CUISINE:

Those whose favorite food is Asian cuisine can hardly do without lemongrass. Its lemony aroma makes it useful not only for fish and chutneys but also in fruit salads and stewed fruit. Very often it is used like bay leaf in cooking. Sweet dishes can be flavored with lemongrass oil, which is industrially produced. Australians make lemongrass tea from *Cymbopogon citratus*, which is a popular, refreshing drink.

HEALTH EFFECTS:

Lemongrass is not only very delicious but also has calming and diuretic effects.

COSMETICS:

Its essential oil is a valuable ingredient for the production of perfumes and soap.

DECORATIVE USES:

For those who like exotic cuisine this combination of exotic spice and decorative houseplant is highly recommended. If you treat the plant well - grow it in good light and keep it well watered and fertilized - it will reward you with a nice aroma all year round. Palmarosa grass leaves have a pleasant rose aroma and can be used for potpourri.

Echinacea purpurea
Echinacea

Type:

Location for growth:

Use:

Features:

FAMILY: Daisy family (*Asteraceae*)

ORIGIN: Echinacea is indigenous to North America, where its shrubs can be found on dry hillsides. Native Americans used it as a medicinal herb.

FEATURES: This shrub, known as red or purple echinacea, was once placed in the rudbeckia genus. The shrub can be 30 - 35 inches tall. Its long, thin leaves are leathery and covered with coarse hair. In summer the plant produces bright purple petals that radiate from brownish-red centers. The blossoms attract bees and butterflies. Its roots in particular contain substances that strengthen the immune system and also have antibiotic affects.

TIP FOR SPECIES: "Alba," "White Luster," and "White Swan" have white flowers, while "Magnus" is known for its large, bright, pinkish-red blossoms and its long blooming period. The "Rubinstern" species has red blossoms.

SIMILAR SPECIES: Thin-leafed *Echinacea angustifolia* also has health effects but can be difficult to grow because it is highly susceptible to excessive moisture. Related species such as

Rudbeckia fulgida, R. Laciniata, and *R. nitida* are very decorative and have light-yellow blossoms.

LOCATION FOR GROWTH: The plant prefers full sun but also tolerates partial shade. It should be grown in soil rich in humus and calcium.

CULTIVATION: In spring it can be sown directly in beds, or if you buy seedlings or young plants, simply divide them. You can also propagate the plants from root shoots. In spring cut the plant back severely.

HARVEST: The richest source of therapeutic substances are the roots. However, flowers, leaves, and stalks can also be used. You can preserve these substances in alcohol, as described below.

A SPECIAL TIP:

TO STRENGTHEN YOUR IMMUNE SYSTEM

Mix equal amounts of dried, chopped echinacea roots with wormwood and peppermint leaves. Pour a cup of boiling water over 2 tablespoonfuls of the mixture and let it steep for 10 minutes, then strain. Drinking 2 – 3 cups a day strengthens your immune system.

To make a tincture, fill a bottle halfway with small pieces of the plant and add 40% alcohol. Close the bottle and store it in a cool, dark place. Shake regularly. Strain the liquid through linen after 2 – 3 weeks. Squeeze well and store the clear tincture in clean, dry bottles.

USE:

HEALTH EFFECTS:

Echinacea has antibiotic properties and also relieves pain. Besides that it can be used to treat injuries. If you wash your injuries with the diluted tincture, you can disinfect them. Used internally it strengthens your immune system and also relieves allergics. If you take 5 – 10 drops of the tincture every 2 - 3 hours at the onset of cold, flu, or sore throat, you can quickly get the symptoms under control. Later you can reduce the dose to 3 times a day until the symptoms disappear.

DECORATIVE USES:

Echinacea's contrasting flowers make the plant very attractive. It is ideal for growing in regular and strip beds. When it is cut and put in a vase it stays fresh for a long time. You can make a nice bouquet by mixing it with grasses, summer and fall asters, phlox, larkspur, alpine fleabane, baby's breath, or Mexican mint.

IMPORTANT PRECAUTION:

People with allergies can suffer from inflammation of the skin or larynx, and asthma. This usually happens if the suggested dose has been exceeded.

Elsholtzia stauntonii
Mint shrub

Type:

Location for growth:

Use:
✗ ❀

FAMILY: Labiates (*Labiatae*)

ORIGIN: Chinese mint shrub originated in northern China where it is known as a culinary herb. Elsewhere, it is grown as a popular ornamental tree.

FEATURES: In summer the shrub can grow to 5 feet. Its thin leaves, which are up to 6 inches long, give off a pleasant aroma reminiscent of caraway, and can be used as a spice. The plants are green and in the fall they turn light purple. The purple-pink, 4 – 8 inch long blooms are very pretty. They produce glistening spikes starting in September.

TIP FOR SPECIES: The 'Alba' species has white blooms and can grow up to 30 inches tall. It is, like the main species, winter hardy.

SIMILAR SPECIES: The annual true or *Vietnamese mint* shrub (Elsholtzia ciliata) has its home in Central Asia, Japan, Korea, and China. In the West, it has only recently been discovered as a culinary herb. Its aroma is reminiscent of lemon. It

blooms in lavender-colored spikes in fall and can be propagated with cuttings.

Location for growth: This species requires a warm, sunny place. It grows perfectly in dry conditions.

Cultivation: *Chinese mint* shrub can be bought in tree nurseries, garden centers, or by mail. Prune the plant in the spring so that it does not grow too tall and maintains its shape. In cold regions it is recommended that you protect the roots with leaves or mulch. This shrub can also be grown in pots. In winter the pots should be insulated to avoid frost damage. The Vietnamese mint shrub is an annual and must be propagated every year.

HARVEST: The aromatic leaves, with their extraordinary smell of caraway and mint, can be harvested throughout the summer.

A SPECIAL TIP:

VIETNAMESE OMELET

Mix 3 eggs with 2 teaspoons Nuoc Mam sauce (available at Asian grocery stores). Heat 1 spoonful of vegetable oil in a pan - preferably a special omelet pan - and pour the egg mixture onto it. Before the mixture sets add 10 peeled shrimp as well as 1 teaspoon finely chopped mint shrub leaves and 1 teaspoon coriander. When the omelet has set put it in the oven to bake for a while. It can be served as a main course or included in a mixed appetizer. When cool it can be cut into strips and eaten like noodles or added to salads and rice dishes.

USE:

CUISINE:

Chopped fresh leaves go well with cucumbers, vegetables, egg dishes, poultry, fish, soups, and sauces. They are a great ingredient in spring rolls. Add to cottage cheese to give it a special flavor.

DECORATIVE USES:

Both species look a bit like sage and brighten any flowerbed with their pinkish-red flowers. Chinese mint shrub can also be grown as a decorative potted plant.

Eruca sativa
Arugula

Type:

Location for growth:

Use:

FAMILY: Mustard family (*Brassicaceae*)

ORIGIN: Arugula grows in the Mediterranean countries and for some time it has been used as a salad green and as an herb.

FEATURES: This annual is also known as true rocket, rocket lettuce, or roquette. It grows quickly and can reach heights of 20 inches. As it is part of the mustard family, it is no wonder that its leaves are rich in mustard oils and vitamin C. In the summer the plant produces yellow-white smooth flowers in loose clusters, and the seeds are used as a spice.

SIMILAR SPECIES: The following examples are not of the *Eruca genus*, but are used the same way in cooking. If you want to obtain a specimen of garlic mustard (*Alliaria petiolata*), do not hesitate to do so. Its smooth spring leaves taste and smell a bit like garlic, and its roots can serve as a substitute for horseradish. The plant grows best in partial shade, in soil rich in nutrients, and it reseeds itself readily. Chopped leaves of home hedge mustard (*Sisymbrium officinale*) give dishes a piquant flavor similar to that of horseradish. You

can also try adding it to cottage cheese and spreading the mixture on bread.

LOCATION FOR GROWTH: This cruciferous plant is best grown in full sun or partial shade. It requires soil rich in nutrients and humus and should be neither excessively wet nor dry.

CULTIVATION: Starting in spring it can be sown either in gardens or on window ledges, where it is grown the same way as cress. If you have a balcony, you can grow it in pots there. When the plants are sufficiently fertilized they grow quickly and are less bitter. However, if you keep the plants too wet, they lose their aroma. When planning vegetable beds, keep in mind that arugula should not be grown next to cabbage family vegetables.

HARVEST: Fresh leaves can be harvested repeatedly - you can either cut off the leaves or the whole plant. If you let some flowers mature they will produce seeds, known as mustard corns.

A SPECIAL TIP:

ARUGULA SALAD WITH MOZZARELLA

Arugula is as closely associated with Italian cuisine as basil. Try the following classic tomato-mozzarella appetizer:
You need 1 – 2 bunches of arugula, some ripe tomatoes (and zucchini if you like,) red onions and mozzarella. Clean the leaves and vegetables, chop the tomatoes and zucchini, slice the onions and cheese and mix. To prepare the dressing, mix 2 tablespoons white wine, 1 tablespoon balsamic vinegar, 1 minced shallot and a crushed clove of garlic. Add 3 tablespoons olive oil and season with salt and pepper before serving.

USE:

CUISINE:

Young, smooth leaves taste good when mixed with cress, mustard, and nuts. Prepared this way they give you a salad rich in vitamins. They also season sauces and cottage cheese. The seeds are used the same way as mustard seeds, for example in pickled vegetables. Oils can also be extracted from them.

HEALTH EFFECTS:

Arugula contains a lot of vitamin C. It has antibacterial properties and also aids digestion.

Foeniculum vulgare
Fennel

Type:

∞ – ☉

Location for growth:

☼

Use:

✕ 🐜 ♈ ✿

Features:

!

FAMILY: Carrot family (*Apicaceae*)

ORIGIN: Wild fennel is indigenous from the Mediterranean to Asia and for ages it has been used as an herb and a spice. Varieties grown in Central Europe, such as sweet fennel and bulb fennel, arose from the wild form.

FEATURES: Sweet fennel (*Foeniculum vulgare var. dulce*) can be a biennial or a perennial. The stalks, which are strong and grooved, produce decorative, feathery leaves. The plant can grow up to 30 – 80 inches tall and produces flower umbels in the summer. The seeds, which taste like anise, come from the umbels and look like small half-moons. Its effects are due to its high essential oil content.

SIMILAR SPECIES: Bulb fennel (*Foeniculum vulgare* var. *azoricum*) is rich in vitamins and tastes good raw, stewed, or baked. Fruit-bearing species do not bloom in summer but produce sturdy bulbs.

LOCATION FOR GROWTH: Fennel demands a warm, sunny place so that the seeds can mature well. The soil should be deep because of fennel's large roots, and at the same time it should contain nutrients and calcium, and be very well tilled.

CULTIVATION: Sweet fennel is a perennial shrub, usually a biennial in northern frost regions. Most species are also suitable as annuals; they should be germinated indoors in February. Otherwise they can be sown outdoors in protected beds, best in rows spaced 8 inches apart. Later thin the plants to 20 inches apart, because the plant grows tall. Until the seeds sprout, the beds should be kept wet. Before winter, cut the stalks back to about 4 inches above the ground and cover the plants with compost or straw. Once grown, fennel easily propagates itself in warm regions.

HARVEST: Young, smooth leaves can be cut off and used fresh in cooking. The seed heads are cut off as soon as the umbels turn brown. When the seeds are covered with gray stripes, they are nearly dry; then they should be hung until fully dry. You can then store them in closed containers.

A SPECIAL TIP:

TEA FOR COUGH AND STOMACH TROUBLES
Before making tea, crush the seeds so that the essential oils can be released. To prepare, pour 1 cup boiling water over one tablespoonful seeds and let steep for 10 minutes. For a cough, drink as much of the hot tea as possible. For stomach and intestinal problems, let the tea steep longer so it is bitter.

USE:

CUISINE:

The seeds and leaves can season fish, salads, and sauces. The seeds can also be used to flavor liqueurs as well as bread and pancakes. Fatty fish becomes easily digestible when fennel is added.

HEALTH EFFECTS:

The seeds are used for a therapeutic tea. It helps with stomach and intestinal problems and also relieves painful flatulence. It can be also used for asthma and whooping cough. Fennel tea is widely used for soothing children.

COSMETICS:

A vapor bath with fennel tea helps if you have dry skin. As the pores are opened by the hot vapor, the skin can absorb the soothing essential oils especially well.

IMPORTANT PRECAUTION:

People with allergies may react to fennel oil with skin or pancreas swelling. Pregnant or nursing women and small children should avoid using concentrated fennel oil.

DECORATIVE USES:

The pretty leaves and large blossom umbels enhance every vegetable bed. There are also very decorative species with bronze leaves and stalks, such as 'Giant Bronze.'

Fragaria vesca
Woodland strawberry

Type:

∞

Location for growth:

☀

··

Use:

✗ 🐜 ♀ ❀

Features:

❗

FAMILY: Rose family (*Rosaceae*)

ORIGIN: Woodland strawberries, the original form of the cultivated strawberry (*Fragaria vesca* var. *hortensis*), can be found throughout the northern hemisphere. In France it was grown as early as the 14th century and since that time many new species have been cultivated. Both wild and cultivated strawberries are popular thanks to their taste and healthful properties.

FEATURES: Strawberry plants take the form of a rosette with trifoliate jagged leaves. They are rich in essential oils, tannins, and flavones. Woodland strawberries bloom and produce fruits until fall, with the main harvest period in June and July. The small fruits contain many vitamins and minerals and an especially large amount of vitamin C.

TIP FOR SPECIES: 'Rügen' and 'Alexandria' are modern wild strawberries without runners. 'Forstina' is a true woodland strawberry which produces a lot of runners. 'Variegata' has creamy-white spots.

SIMILAR SPECIES: Decorative strawberries, such as the pink-blooming 'Pink Panda,' were cultivated as hybrids of woodland strawberry and Shrubby Cinquefoil (Potentilla).

LOCATION FOR GROWTH: Woodland and wild strawberries require a natural place - it should be partially shaded with soil rich in nutrients and humus. They grow well among trees, whereas the fruits turn leathery in full sun.

CULTIVATION: Can be germinated in pots in mid-March. The seeds can be obtained from gardeners, garden centers, or via post. Since the seeds are very fine, they should be spread on top of the soil and not covered. The seedlings can be thinned later in the pots and planted outdoors from the middle of May. Besides seeds, you can also buy seedlings. Wild strawberries can also be grown on balconies. If you want to avoid undesirable propagation through runners in your garden, growing them in boxes is recommended. The harvest may be speeded up if you cut off the first flowers.

HARVEST: The leaves can be picked throughout the whole vegetation period, but make sure you do not cut off so many leaves that the plant can't survive. Before you use the leaves, dry them in the shade. The fruits have the strongest aroma when mature. They are quite small and you will need to pick many of them to have enough, but they will make up for this with their sweet strawberry flavor.

A SPECIAL TIP:

SUMMER STRAWBERRY PUNCH
Put 2 pounds wild strawberries in a bowl with 4 ounces powdered sugar and enough white wine to cover. Let sit for about 30 minutes. Then add chilled white wine (a total of 3 bottles). Just before serving, add 1 bottle sparkling wine and let the celebration begin!

USE:

CUISINE:

Strawberries taste good raw, in rhubarb compote, with cakes, ice cream, pudding, or in drinks.

HEALTH EFFECTS:

Tea made from dried leaves helps with stomach and intestinal problems and strengthens the immune system. It can also be used as a gargle that soothes mucous membranes. To prepare this mixture pour 1 cup water over two teaspoons dried leaves.

COSMETICS:

Cleansing lotion made from fresh pressed leaves soothes the skin, especially if it is sunburned. You can also put pieces of strawberries on sunburned skin. A creamy mask made from strawberries with some cream and honey relieves dry, damaged skin. However, use only if you are not allergic to strawberries.

DECORATIVE USES:

Woodland and wild strawberries are ideal for half shade among rows of trees, producing a decorative look. They can be also grown in balcony pots or flower columns.

IMPORTANT PRECAUTION:

People with allergies can suffer from an itchy rash after eating or using strawberries.

Galium odoratum
Sweet woodruff

Type:
∞

Location for growth:
☀ – ☼

Use:
✗ 𝕬 ✿

Features:
!

FAMILY: *Rubiceae*

ORIGIN: Sweet woodruff has its home in nearly all wooded regions, from Iran to Siberia. For more than 1,000 years it has been a basic ingredient of the traditional May punch-bowl. That is why it is also called May plant or Mayflower in many languages.

FEATURES: This perennial shrub produces creeping roots from which square-sectioned stalks grow in spring, up to 12 inches tall. The lance-shaped leaves are characteristic, located on the stalk in star shapes, at intervals. In May the plant produces white, fragrant blossoms in umbels. The typical aroma of sweet woodruff comes from the cumarin contained in the plant, and is especially strong when the plants wilt and are dried. Besides that, the plant contains a lot of vitamin C, tannins, and alkaloids.

SIMILAR SPECIES: Torino sweet woodruff (*Asperula taurina*), also called Torino Meier, has a much more intense aroma than its relative, and used to be classified as a species of *Asperula*. The flowers give every bouquet a beautiful aroma.

Location for growth: The plant requires partial or full shade. Loose, wet earth rich in humus is also very important.

Cultivation: Sowing is possible in fall but demands a lot of patience. It is easier to obtain seedlings, which can be planted outdoors and then spread very quickly. However, give the plant some time before you start harvesting the leaves. During long dry periods give sweet woodruff extra water.

HARVEST: The plant is harvested before blooming from May to June. When dried the aroma is much more intense.

A SPECIAL TIP:

SWEET WOODRUFF PUNCHBOWL
There are many variants of this May drink. Below are some of them:
Mix 2 bunches sweet woodruff together with half a cup wine brandy, 2 ounces sugar, 1 box of vanilla sugar, and 1 bottle of white wine. Let sit for about 2 hours. Then remove the sweet woodruff and add 3 bottles chilled white wine and a bottle of sparkling wine. Make sure the stalks do not sit in the liquid. If you like, you can add peppermint, pimpernel, or other herbs to flavor the bowl. Another recommendation for this drink is to mix one part rosé wine and one part white wine instead of using just white wine. If you want to prepare the bowl without any alcohol you can use fruit juice and sparkling mineral water.

USE:

CUISINE:

The classic use of sweet woodruff is in preparation of the May bowl. It is also used for "Berliner Weiße" and "Götterspeise." The plant can be used for preparing tea or as an ingredient in marmalades, juices, and ices, to give them extra aroma. Tip: To add the aroma of sweet woodruff to drinks, allow a bunch of it to sit in the desired liquid for one hour.

HEALTH EFFECTS:

Tea made from dried leaves helps with nervousness and insomnia. At the same time it also cleanses the blood. Small bags of dried plants placed in your wardrobe should repel moths. In the past, it was added to pillows to ward off insomnia.

IMPORTANT PRECAUTION:

Sweet woodruff should be used with care because of its high cumarin content which can result in discomfort and headaches.

DECORATIVE USES:

Sweet woodruff is a decorative, steadily-blooming plant that grows under trees. That is why it can be grown together with grasses and ferns. It is suitable for planting on plains. However it quickly spreads, so keep the plant under control. On the other hand, sweet woodruff keeps out weeds, thanks to its root system.

Gentiana lutea
Yellow gentian

Type:
☉

Location for growth:
☼ – ☼

Use:
✕ 🜨 ✿

Features:
!

FAMILY: Gentian family (*Gentianaceae*)

ORIGIN: The yellow gentian comes from the mountainous regions of southern and central Europe. It grows not only in mountain meadows but also on rocky heights where there is soil containing calcium. The plant is grown in huge quantities because their roots are used industrially for the production of liqueurs.

FEATURES: This shrub is a higher-altitude species of gentian, and grows in soil containing calcium. The plant can grow up to 4 feet tall. Its strong stalks produce yellow flower-spikes in the summer. The strong roots contain many bitter alkaloids and tannins which support digestion, and are used as a basic ingredient in many well-known liqueurs and medical tinctures.

SIMILAR SPECIES: The root extract of Tibetan gentian (*Gentiana tibetica*) is used in traditional Chinese medicine for treating liver ailments. You can get the seeds in specialist shops. Cross gentian (*G. cruciata*) tolerates dry conditions and is a favorite with fans of rock gardens. Its name was

derived from its leaves, which are arranged in crosses. In the past it was believed to protect against pest infestations. The blue-flowered species, such as the willow gentian (*G. ascle-piadea*), are especially decorative but less suitable for use in cooking and medicine.

LOCATION FOR GROWTH: This wild shrub requires a sunny place and deep soil rich in nutrients.

CULTIVATION: You can buy young plants or start the seeds in pots in late winter and plant outdoors in spring. If you sow the seeds outdoors in fall they should be well covered.

It is worth noting that the seeds require a cool period for sprouting. If you wish to harvest the roots and use them, you need patience, as they will only be ready for harvest after an average of 5 years. Fortunately, all the other parts of the plant also contain the precious bitter substances.

Harvest: The leaves can be continuously harvested throughout the growing period, while the roots are harvested from September to April. Both are used dried.

A special tip:

Yellow gentian tea strengthens the heart and improves blood circulation

Pour 1 cup boiling water over 1 teaspoon chopped dried roots. Allow to steep for 5 minutes and then strain. The tea should be consumed lukewarm before meals.

Gentian tea, effective against heartburn

Pour boiling water over 1 teaspoon yellow gentian leaves. Allow to steep for 10 minutes in an open cup and then strain. Drink lukewarm. Drinking 2–3 cups a day effectively relieves heartburn.

USE:

CUISINE:
The roots are used in herbal spirits to stimulate digestion and the production of gastric acids.

HEALTH EFFECTS:
The dried roots and leaves are used for tea, cold extracts, and tincture. The bitter substances stimulate the secretion of gastric acids and therefore stimulate the appetite and digestion. The roots are an important ingredient in Swedish herbal mixtures. Yellow gentian has strengthening effects and was once used to expel worms in people and animals.

DECORATIVE USES:
With its yellow flower-spikes the yellow gentian fits best in beds with wild shrubs. It also grows well in the light shade of trees, and attracts nectar-gathering insects.

IMPORTANT PRECAUTION:

Because of its high alkaloid content, pregnant and nursing women should avoid yellow gentian tea. Patients suffering from gastric and intestinal diseases should take care when using gentian preparations.

Helichrysum italicum
Curry plant

Type:

Location for growth:

☼

Use:

FAMILY: Daisy family (*Asteraceae*)

ORIGIN: The curry plant, also known as Italian immortelle, originally came from southwestern Europe. With its curry-like aroma, it has been growing in popularity as a culinary herb.

FEATURES: The curry plant grows in its place of origin as an evergreen shrub. It has a height ranging from 15 to 20 inches and its spikes become woody in the second year. The silvery-gray leaves, which resemble nails, contain a lot of essential oil. During the summer the plant produces small, white blossom heads, and in the winter it can withstand frost up to 14°F if planted in a suitable place.

TIP FOR SPECIES: The white-leafed spice 'White Wonder' (also known as the snow curry plant) is used as a spice for rice, poultry, and fish.

SIMILAR SPECIES: *Helichrysum italicum* subsp. *serotinum*, a subspecies of the traditional curry plant, grows in a more compact form and produces smaller leaves. In shops you can

get it under the name "dwarf curry plant." *H. stoechas* produces leaves similar to lavender and tea made from it was once used to fight respiratory infections, because it released phlegm. A tea made from the leaves and flowers of *H. arenarium* (also known as sand immortelle) soothes and strengthens the stomach. The curry plant is not identical to the curry-leaf plant (*Murraya koenigii*), which comes from southern Asia. The leaves of M. koenigii are also used for curry dishes. In specialist shops you can buy them as "curry leaves" or "neem leaves."

PLACE TO GROW: As with all plants in this family, curry plant requires good sun and dry soil. It will only produce its typical silver-gray colored leaves if grown in such a place, and will also be more frost resistant.

CULTIVATION: The curry plant can be obtained in specialist garden centers. It should be cut back after it flowers so it will grow into a shrub. You can propagate the plants yourselves with cuttings; 3 cuttings planted in a 5-inch pot produce a rich bouquet. The young plants should be pinched back after rooting so that it will produce more branches. During the growing period the fertilizer should contain nitrogen; otherwise the plants will not turn green.

HARVEST: The leaves can be repeatedly cut and used for cooking. They should be added to dishes 10 minutes before serving, and then removed just before serving.

A SPECIAL TIP:

THE FOLLOWING MIXTURE HELPS WITH AGITATED STATES
A mixture of equal quantities of lemon oil, tangerine oil and curry plant oil has calming effects if ingested in small quantities. When applied to the skin it smoothes out wrinkles and scars and if you immediately use the mixture on boils, it prevents swelling. You can get the oils at a pharmacy or specialist shop.

USE:

CUISINE:

With their mild curry aroma, the leaves flavor soups, sauces, vegetables, rice, and fish. You can use a whole stalk for cooking and then remove before serving. You can also mix the plants together with rosemary, sage, and thyme and crush them in a mortar, then add oil and season with salt and pepper. Apply this mixture to fish fillets, wrap in aluminum foil and put on the grill. The curry plant is an ingredient in many herbal mixtures.

HEALTH EFFECTS:

Tea made from curry plant relieves stomachaches and helps with asthma. If you rub it over boils it relieves pain and at the same time clears the skin.

DECORATIVE USES:

Curry plant is a very pretty plant thanks to its silver-gray branches. It is a spring plant suitable for growing in balcony pots. The blossom umbels are also suitable for dried bouquets. The dwarf curry plant can be grown in beds or used for trimming paths.

Hypericum perforatum
Saint John's Wort

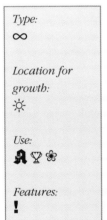

Type:
∞

Location for growth:
☼

Use:
𝕬 ♍ ❀

Features:
!

FAMILY: *Clusiaceae*

ORIGIN: St John's wort is indigenous to Europe, northern Africa and Asia. Its soothing effects on the soul and body have long been known. In the past the plant was used as protection against diseases and evil powers.

FEATURES: This thick-branched shrub (also called spotted St John's wort) can grow up to 3 feet tall. Its most notable characteristic is its leaves, which contain oil. If you hold the leaves against light they seem to be full of holes - an appearance caused by small cells filled with oil. The bright, gold-yellow flowers serve as a beautiful decoration. They bloom in high summer and also contain a red dye. Leaves and blossoms contain hypericin, which has anti-depressant properties. The leaves also contain essential oils, tannins, and anti-oxidant flavonoids.

SIMILAR SPECIES: Tutsam (*Hypericum androsaemum*) has similar medicinal benefits as St John's wort, and displays an attractive red color during the fall. Its orange-red fruits are popular in bouquets. Aaron's beard (*H. calycinum*) is

a strong, blooming plant which can be used as ground-cover.

LOCATION FOR GROWTH: A warm, sunny place is very important to enable the plant to produce its valuable substances. The soil should be well-tilled and dry rather than wet. If grown in soil containing a lot of calcium, the leaves turn yellow.

CULTIVATION: St John's wort can be obtained as young plants or seeds. The seeds should be germinated indoors during the winter, in small pots to save you time separating them. In late spring they can be planted outdoors in a good location. Make sure you do not plant them too close together. Spacing of 8 inches is recommended. Add organic fertilizer as well as compost. Remember to cover the plants with enough soil so that you can harvest them from year to year. Older plants can be separated. It is also possible to propagate the plant with cuttings.

Harvest: The stalks should be cut back in full bloom and bound into bunches and hung to dry. Blossoms and leaves can be preserved in oil.

A special tip

St John's wort tincture
Crush half an ounce of fresh blossoms in a mortar and add 2 ounces of 70% alcohol. Steep for 10 days before straining and decanting into dark bottles. If 10 – 15 drops are taken with 1 teaspoon water for about 2 months it helps with nervousness, exhaustion, and psychological problems. For boils, spread with the tincture and massage it in, but be careful because it contains alcohol and therefore stings in open wounds. St John's wort oil has the same effects. To make the oil, cover about 4 ounces of crushed blossoms with olive oil and store in a sunny place for 6 weeks. Shake daily. As soon as the oil turns red, strain and decant into dark bottles. One spoonful taken daily for 4–6 weeks will strengthen your psyche and performance.

USE:

HEALTH EFFECTS:

If prepared as tea and consumed for several weeks the plant helps with nervousness and depression. To prepare 1 cup of this tea, pour boiling water over 2 teaspoons dried leaves and blossoms. St John's wort also improves circulation and digestion. Taken internally it relieves stomach upsets.

COSMETICS:

Saint John's wort oil is used as a bath additive, for its antiseptic and soothing effects. It makes your skin smooth and pliable when it is used as soap. A natural yellow or orange dye is produced from the flowers.

DECORATIVE USES:

Saint John's wort is a real beauty, with its yellow glistening blossoms, which appear during Indian summer. However, the decorative varieties are less effective for medicines.

IMPORTANT PRECAUTION:

The hypericin makes skin more sensitive, so do not take risks. Avoid direct sunshine and tanning parlors after use. Also, contact with the plant during sunny days may result in skin irritation for those who are susceptible to rashes.

Hyssopus officinalis
Hyssop

Type:

Location for growth:

Use:

FAMILY: Labiate family (*Lamiaceae*)

ORIGIN: Hyssop originates in the south of Europe and in Asia. It has been used as an antiseptic for thousands of years, and this function is even mentioned in the Old Testament. It was monks who began to grow hyssop in monastery gardens. The aromatic herb was also used to freshen rooms.

FEATURES: This evergreen grows as a shrub to a height of 12 - 25 inches. The leaves, which contain many oil glands, grow close to each other and spread their shoots .The scented flowers, filled with nectar, attract bees in the summer, which is why the plant is sometimes called "bee herb." It is the essential oils, tannins, and bitter alkaloids that make this plant so valuable.

TIP FOR SPECIES: The blue-violet "Rosea" type has pink flowers and "Alba" has white ones.

LOCATION FOR GROWTH: Hyssop likes sunny places with dry, loose, lime-rich soil, which should also be deep enough to accommodate the long roots.

CULTIVATION: For domestic use, buy one or two young plants at the beginning of the year. You can cut larger plants back and root the cuttings. It should be started in early spring at home and in May can be planted, spaced 8 to 12 inches apart. Hyssop is also well suited for planting in pots. It tolerates dry conditions and should be protected from freezing in very cold winters. Dried parts of the plant should be cut off in spring or if necessary the whole plant should be cut back. Otherwise, the plant is easy to care for.

HARVEST: The leaves and tops of the young shoots can be gathered and added to dishes fresh.

Be careful with seasoning if you are not used to hyssop, because it has a bitter taste. The flowering shoots can also be dried and stored. The aroma is best just before the buds open.

A SPECIAL TIP:

COLOR AND SCENT

You get a really unusual decoration by adding hyssop to arrangements of plants that bloom in different colors. You can create groups of coherent types such as "all pink," or you can plant small hedges. The plants look really great sown among roses.

USE:

CUISINE:

Fresh hyssop is used for seasoning salads, sauces and meat and fish dishes. You can make rich dishes more healthful by adding hyssop. You can also use it for making a delicious herbal cottage cheese or herbal oil, and the taste of hyssop liqueur is well worth experiencing.

HEALTH EFFECTS:

Hyssop is especially famous for its disinfectant properties, thanks to its essential oil. It strengthens and stimulates digestion and boosts the immune system in general. It is also used for coughs; hyssop tea helps loosen phlegm. It soothes a sore throat when gargled. To make a cup of tea, cover 2 teaspoons of the herb with boiling water, and allow to cool for 5 minutes.

COSMETICS:

Hyssop is often used for making perfumes and potpourris.

DECORATIVE USES:

The tender flowers not only attract people, but also many bees. You can plant hyssop in hedges or in groups in locations with mild winters.

Inula helenium
Elecampane

Type:
☉

Location for growth:
☼ – ☀

Use:
✕ 🐜 ♈ ✿

Features:
❗

FAMILY: Composites (*Asteraceae*)

ORIGIN: This plant is indigenous to the Mediterranean as well as parts of central Asia. The ancient Greeks and Romans used it as a therapeutic plant and a dye. The crusaders brought it into northern climes, where it was planted in rural gardens. We can find this herb even today in damp meadows, near graves or along paths.

FEATURES: The herb can reach a height of 6 feet. Its egg-shaped leaves are up to 20 inches long and its large yellow blossoms shine in summer. It has strong, beetlike roots, which are of medical importance because they are rich in essential oils, elecampane camphor, inulin and saponin, as well as resins and alkaloids.

SIMILAR SPECIES: Swordleaf inula (*Inula ensifolia*) is classified as an inula, but it has no medical importance. It is often used decoratively in gardens and bees like its beautiful, opulent blossoms. Rock gardeners often plant it.

LOCATION FOR GROWTH: Elecampane likes sun and partial shade and its roots prefer shade as well. The ground must be rich and deep and must contain clay for the plant to grow properly. The ground should be slightly damp, but not wet.

CULTIVATION: You can buy seedlings and plant them from April. Later they need to be thinned to 25 inches apart. Large shrubs can be split after they bloom.

HARVEST: Carefully separate the roots in fall. It is usual to gather some of the plant's roots instead of the whole bunch. Choose the roots very carefully, so that the plant can grow back. Wash the roots, dry them and cut them into pieces. You can hang them on strings to dry or put them in the oven heated no hotter than 100°F, so that none of the essential oil is lost. The dried roots are used for making tea or alcohol infusions.

A SPECIAL TIP:

FACE LOTION AND HAIR RINSE

Boil 2 tablespoons crushed elecampane roots for 10 minutes in a cup of water, and then set aside for one hour. Apply it frequently during the day to distressed skin. You can also use it, after it has been cooled and filtered, as a rinse for dry hair. This rinse should not be used on blond hair.

USE:

CUISINE:

The dried roots are used to add aroma to sweet dishes. It is used in small amounts because of its bitter taste. Tea can be made from elecampane roots, using 1 teaspoon of root for 1 cup of tea.

HEALTH EFFECTS:

Elecampane's antiseptic and digestion-supporting properties make it a highly prized plant. It is a useful remedy for coughs, bronchitis, and asthma, because it loosens phlegm. The roots contain the important polysaccharide inulin. Elecampane is used industrially in the production of bitter liqueurs, cough medicines and digestive aids.

COSMETICS:

Elecampane root extract is used on eczema and rashes because it helps to soothe irritated patches of skin.

DECORATIVE USES:

Elecampane serves well as a background in border beds. Both groups and individual plants are very pretty when used decoratively.

IMPORTANT PRECAUTION:

Excessive amounts of elecampane can cause discomfort and vomiting. Drink no more than 2 – 4 cups of tea per day and note the advice on proper use.

Laurus nobilis
Laurel (Bay leaf)

Type:

⊙

Location for growth:

☼ – ☼

Use:

✗ ♔ ❀

Features:

❗

FAMILY: Bay leaf (*Lauraceae*)

ORIGIN: Laurel (the plant is called laurel, but its leaves are known as bay leaves) originated in Asia, but is widespread in the Mediterranean. You can find laurel growing in groves on the Canary Islands. The laurel wreath was a classical symbol of success and achievement, especially among Olympic athletes, successful army leaders and well-known poets hence term "laureate" is derived from this honor.

FEATURES: This evergreen shrub can develop into a 30-foot tree. Cold climates do not suit laurel and it is usually planted in pots and rarely grows to its potential height. The flowers are small and white with developed black berries. Laurel is a heterogeneous plant, so to propagate it you will need both the male and female types. Bay leaves have wavy edges and an aromatic scent, which derives from their rich essential oil.

LOCATION FOR GROWTH: Laurel needs full sun or partial shade to grow well. It prefers a place protected from wind, and the soil must be rich.

CULTIVATION: You can plant your own laurel as seedlings or buy the plant in a shop. It is usually planted in pots and needs regular watering and rich fertilizer, especially in the summer. Additionally, add some dry substrate from time to time. Laurel has to hibernate in a dark place at 9 - 104°F. Late frosts are especially dangerous and can damage the shoots. It can be planted and pruned into many different shapes, such as a pyramid. The best time for pruning is spring.

HARVEST: You can gather bay leaves throughout the year if your plant is growing in a pot. Even plants that are two years old have the same aroma and dark green leaves. You can dry the leaves in the shade, but the aroma fades.

A special tip:

Bay vinegar

Place 1 washed laurel shoot (approximately 10 – 15 leaves) and 1 teaspoon fennel seeds in a clean, glass bottle (wine-bottle sized). Then pour in apple-cider vinegar so that all the leaves are immersed. No mold should appear! Seal the glass firmly and store it in a dark, cool place for 2 weeks.

USE:

CUISINE:

Bay leaves are used to season soups, sauces, fish, and meat dishes. Add the leaves (without the stem) to the dish during preparation and remove it before serving. Bay leaves add a delicious flavor to pickled olives or cheese.

HEALTH EFFECTS:

Laurel oil is used for treating sprains and bruises - apply to the injured area. Laurel fruits are used to treat rheumatism.

DECORATIVE USES:

This plant graces balconies, terraces, and winter gardens with its scented evergreen leaves. You can arrange a beautiful herb garden with other herbs of the Mediterranean, such as rosemary, myrtle, lavender, and oregano. These plants can grow in terracotta or stone pots.

IMPORTANT PRECAUTION:

When used externally laurel oil can cause allergic reactions, as can the leaves when used in cooking. Laurel can be narcotic when taken in vast quantities and it can cause the loss of consciousness, for example if you drink too much laurel tea.

Lavandula angustifolia
Lavender

Type:

∞

Location for growth:

☼

Use:

✗ ♫ ♉ ✿

Features:

!

FAMILY: *Lamiaceae*

ORIGIN: Originally, lavender was indigenous to the Mediterranean area, and its history is long and rich. The Romans used it in baths and also against headaches. To create a pleasant scent in a room, people simply laid its leaves on the floor. Nowadays, lavender is widely grown in Provence and is used in the production of perfumes and soaps.

FEATURES: Lavender grows to 15 - 25 inches and has aromatic leaves with silvery-gray hairs. Scented flowers appear on long ears starting in July. The plant is rich in essential oils, saponins, tannins, and alkaloids.

TIP FOR SPECIES: "Hidcote Blue" remains only 12 inches high. Its early flowers are a bright violet-blue, and give off an intense scent. The pendant "Hidcote Pink" has pink flowers, as does "Loddon Pink". "Grappenhall" and "Munstead" have blue flowers, and "Nana Alba" white.

SIMILAR SPECIES: French scented lavender (*Lavandula x intermedia*) is a cross of *L.angustifolia* and *L.latifolia*. This

type richly adorns the fields of Provence. The violet-blue types "Dutch," "Blue Dwarf," and "Grosso" are famously well-growing plants.

LOCATION FOR GROWTH: Lavender needs sun and shelter from wind. The ground should be slightly moist and contain clay.

CULTIVATION: Lavender can be started indoors in spring, or starting in May it can be planted in gardens. Plants should be spaced at 20-inch intervals, but it is easier and faster to buy young plants in the shops, where you can find many types.

The plants should be cut back by two-thirds after blooming so that they will bloom again. You can also take cuttings or cut back the whole plant. You should cover the plant if the winter weather becomes too cold. The dry shoots are cut back in spring.

HARVEST: The young shoots can be used until the beginning of the blooming period, but the flowers are more interesting. Cut them off in mid-bloom and hang them to dry; they will then keep their scent intact.

A SPECIAL TIP:

LAVENDER WINE, WHICH IMPROVES CONCENTRATION
Boil 1 tablespoon lavender flowers for a short time in a pint of wine. Let it cool and drink it in small amounts before and after each meal.

USE:

CUISINE:
You can use lavender in fish and meat dishes as well as in sweet dishes. Lavender is one of the famous "Herbes de Provence," along with hyssop, oregano, basil, rosemary, sage, thyme, and fennel.

HEALTH EFFECTS:
Lavender is used as a bath ingredient to induce sleep and relieve stress. It helps with tension and stomachaches. You can use a pillow with lavender for better sleep; you can also put some in your wardrobe to repel moths. To relieve headaches and stress symptoms, use lavender oil in an aroma lamp.

COSMETICS:
Dried lavender is used as a bath ingredient, and oil is also extracted from them.

DECORATIVE USES:
Lavender looks good with roses. You can put it next to plants on the edges of flowerbeds, and the scent reaches even the highest balconies.

IMPORTANT PRECAUTION:

The flowers are invaluable, but as lavender oil is used internally to purify the stomach and intestines it can cause dizziness and possible loss of consciousness, so pregnant women should avoid taking it in large amounts.

Lepidium sativum
Garden cress

Type:
∞

Location for growth:

Use:

FAMILY: Mustard family (*Brassicaceae*)

ORIGIN: Cresses originated in Asia, where they have been used for centuries. They were placed in the graves of pharaohs as gifts. The Romans regarded garden cress as a culinary herb with great health benefits.

FEATURES: Cress is cultivated annually. It can reach a height of 12 - 20 inches if you do not cut it back. The lower leaves are round or oval; the upper leaves are broad and round or pinnate. Cresses have delicate white or red flowers in summer. They are rich in vitamin C, minerals and carotene mustard oils, which gives them a peppery, pungent flavor.

SPECIAL TIPS: Cresses with large, wide or feathered leaves enhance many dishes.

SIMILAR SPECIES: Broadleafed pepperweed (*Lepidium latifolium*) originated in northeastern Europe and now grows in other areas with similar climates as a perennial. Its leaves and roots have a peppery flavor similar to that of the cress.

LOCATION FOR GROWTH: Cress does best in partial shade; if the climate is too hot, it needs full shade. It often wilts in direct sunlight when it is very hot. The ground should be well tilled and quite moist.

CULTIVATION: The plant can grow in window boxes or in greenhouses throughout the year, but you should wait until the beginning of March before planting cress in the ground. The seeds should be put deep into the ground, slightly pressed in but not covered with soil. They germinate in two days and grow quite quickly into young plants. You must water regularly. You can enjoy fresh cress all year if you plant new seedlings every 7 - 14 days. When planting outside, choose different places for each planting. The roots may be damaged when cress is planted in the same place.

HARVEST: The leaves should be gathered when they are young and 3 - 4 inches tall. This usually occurs ten days after planting. They lose their usefulness when the plant blooms. You can also gather seedlings and flowers and use them as a flavor or garnish for foods.

SPECIAL TIP:

CRESS HEDGEHOG

You will have vitamin C all year if you grow cress. In order to have a steady supply of fresh herbs, plant new seedlings every week. You can also plant them in a decorative hedgehog - which is both pretty and practical. You need a clay hedgehog, which you soak in water for 30 minutes before planting the seeds in its holes. Then water it daily to keep the seedlings damp. The plants then grow quickly and thickly in the shape of a hedgehog.

USE:

CUISINE:

Cress is always used fresh. The pungent flavor is well suited for salads, raw foods, and cottage cheese, as well as with cabbage or cold meats. You can use the leaves in very small amounts when making sandwiches, soups, or sauces. They are used in the well-known Frankfurter Green Sauce.

HEALTH EFFECTS:

Cress is rich in vitamin C throughout the year. It purifies the blood, and stimulates digestion and the urinary tract. It is especially suitable for detoxing.

Levisticum officinale
Lovage

Type:
⊙

Location for
growth:
☼ – ☀

Use:
✗ 𝕽 ♈ ✿

Features:
!

FAMILY: Parsley family (*Apiaceae*)

ORIGIN: Lovage originated in ancient Persia and its current home is in the Mediterranean area. Monks brought the so-called "almighty medicament" to central and western Europe.

FEATURES: The shoots can grow up to 6 feet tall. The plant has a squared, hollow shoot, which spreads into branches and very large pinnate leaves higher up. Yellow-green umbels appear on the sturdy shoots. The plant contains an essential oil that is used as the main ingredient in the production of Maggi (a widely used European stock flavoring), which is why this plant is sometimes called "Maggi Herb" in Germany. It also contains tannins and alkaloids.

LOCATION FOR GROWTH: Lovage grows in full sun and partial shade, but it needs a lot of space. The soil should be deep, rich, and damp. The plant does not like extreme wetness.

CULTIVATION: One or two large plants are usually sufficient for home use. You can buy young plants to save time

sowing, but if you enjoy the sowing part, the best time is in March. Plant the seeds in a flowerbed and thin later so the strongest plants are spaced about 20 inches apart. Lovage needs a consistently damp place; otherwise it is easy to care for. To make the leaves even stronger, cut off the flowers. Store the plant in a cool place during the winter. You can cut the roots back if they spread too widely, and the plant can be separated until the roots are too deep underground.

HARVEST: You can gather the leaves the whole summer and use them fresh or dried. Cut the plant back to approximately 4 inches above the ground and it will grow back quickly. The roots are also used for seasoning foods.

SPECIAL TIP:

VEGETABLE SOUP WITH LOVAGE
Saute 2 minced onions in butter and olive oil. Then add 2 teaspoons lovage leaves and saute again. Stir in 1 tablespoon flour and slowly pour in 1½ pints vegetable broth. Cook the soup for a short time, add salt, pepper, and nutmeg, and then cook for 10 more minutes. Prior to serving add half a cup of whipped cream and serve with baked breadsticks.

USE:

CUISINE:

The leaves and roots add a delicious flavor to soups, salads, vegetables, meats, and fish. The amount should be carefully measured because of the intense flavor. It has an even richer aroma when dried. Sprigs are used to add aroma to liqueurs, and they are also used in perfumes.

HEALTH EFFECTS:

Lovage strengthens the urinary system and stimulates digestion. It helps with flatulence and painful heartburn. Lovage tea is used for breathing difficulties and as a general tonic. 2 - 3 cups of tea should help with migraine problems. To prepare the tea, boil 2 teaspoons chopped roots in 1 cup water and then set aside.

COSMETICS:

A lovage bath will soothe skin inflammations. To keep your feet from sweating, pour a pint of hot water over a handful of the fresh herb. After it has cooled, use it in a footbath.

DECORATIVE USES:

Lovage is an impressive herb with a distinctive scent.

IMPORTANT ADVICE:

Using lovage to excess can harm the kidneys and cause dizziness. It should not be taken during pregnancy.

Malva sylvestris
Mallow

Type:

Location for growth:

Use:

FAMILY: Mallow (*Malvaceae*)

ORIGIN: Wild mallow is common from the Mediterranean area to subtropical Asia. It was used as a therapeutic herb and a vegetable by the Romans and Greeks. Nowadays it can be found throughout Europe as a typical garden plant.

FEATURES: Mallow grows to a height of 3 feet. It is somewhat feathery, with long, palm-shaped leaves. The pinkish-violet ribbed flowers appear all summer, and contain the natural pigment malvin. The plant is valuable for the various expectorant substances it contains, and it is used as an ingredient for cough syrup. It is also known as cheese-mallow.

SPECIAL TIPS: The wild form of this plant has been used to breed other types, which differ mainly by their flowers. Primley Blue has low, blue flowers, Brave Heart's flowers are 35 inches high, and Cottenham Blue has light blue flowers.

SIMILAR SPECIES: The leaves of musk mallow (*Malva moschata*) are famous for their musky scent. Its flowers are

pink, and those of the 'Alba' type are white. Rose mallow (*m. alcea*) has big, pastel pink flowers. Both types can be used in cooking and for making therapeutic products.

LOCATION FOR GROWTH: Mallow prefers warm, sunny places, partial shade, and rich, well-aerated soil.

CULTIVATION: The wild plant is sown directly in the soil in the fall. It reseeds itself. You can also buy young plants and take cuttings from overgrown plants during the summer. Mallow likes any soil, but it does best in sandy, well-watered soil. Rich soil makes the plant grow faster.

HARVEST: The leaves and flowers can be gathered in summer. They keep best and longest if they are dried. After drying the flowers turn dark blue.

SPECIAL TIP:

COMPRESSES FOR SKIN INFLAMMATION
Boil 1 tablespoon flowers and leaves in 1 quart water for 10 minutes. Let it cool and then soak a towel in it. Hold it against the irritated place on your skin for 10 minutes.

HEALING TEA AND GARGLE IN ONE
To prepare tea, pour 1 cup hot water over 2 teaspoons flowers and leaves. Set it aside for one day. It is then ready for drinking or gargling. A tea mixture of mallow, lime, and camelia flowers helps fight the flu.

USE:

CUISINE:

The leaves are prepared like spinach and are good as a side dish. In the past a puree of the plant was served to children to improve their digestion.

HEALTH EFFECTS:

This plant is suitable for treating inflammations and purging the body, and is helpful for expelling phlegm. It is especially useful for relieving an irritating cough or bronchitis, and it also strengthens the stomach and stimulates digestion. It is used in the form of tea or as a bath ingredient, but it should not be combined with tea made from hibiscus leaves.

DECORATIVE USES:

Wild mallow blooms steadily until fall. It looks good in natural gardens and is especially suitable for herbal flowerbeds. It can decorate any fence. Planting this protected wild herb in your garden supports the conservation of wild species.

Matricaria recutita
Chamomile

Type:
∞

Location for growth:
☼

Use:

Features:
!

FAMILY: Composites (*Asteraceae*)

ORIGIN: Chamomile's original home was in southeastern Europe and northern Asia, but it has spread throughout Europe. Its therapeutic effects have been known for thousands of years. It was used to treat female ailments, which is why it is sometimes called "Mother Herb." There is a superstition that this plant has miraculous effects. It was hung in a bunch in a room, and if the bunch moved when a woman walked in, then the woman was marked as a witch.

FEATURES: Chamomile grows in shrubs to a height of 8 - 20 inches. The pinnate leaves give off a strong scent. It blooms all summer. The daisy-like yellow and white flowers are typical features of the original chamomile. They exude a very strong scent, and are hollow when you break them open. The leaves contain glucoside, cumarin, bitter alkaloids, and an essential oil which becomes blue after distillation.

SIMILAR SPECIES: Carpet chamomile (*Tripleurospermum caucasica, earlier Matricaria caucasica*) covers the ground with its pretty flowers. Roman chamomile (*Chamaemelum nobile*)

has a fresh scent and health effects similar to those of common chamomile.

LOCATION FOR GROWTH: To create the best conditions for this plant, which is rich in valuable substances, plant it in a sunny place with rich soil. It is easy to grow.

CULTIVATION: Young plants grow fast when they are started in seed boxes in early spring. The seedlings should be only slightly pushed into the ground and not covered with soil. Water well. At the end of April they should be planted, spaced 8 inches apart. You can also plant them in pots. Fertilize chamomile carefully; otherwise it grows too quickly, with fewer flowers. Once they have been sown once, the next sowing is easier.

HARVEST: You can gather the flowers until fall and use them fresh or dried. You get the greatest amount of valuable substances from the third to the fifth day after blooming. To catch the best time for harvesting, check your plants every day. Dry the flowers in a shaded place.

SPECIAL TIP:

FIRST AID FOR YOUR PETS

If your dog, cat, etc., suffers from diarrhea, give it warm chamomile tea to drink instead of water. Prepare it by boiling 1 - 2 tablespoons of the flowers in one cup water for 10 minutes, and then set it aside to cool. You can also make compresses with the tea to treat eye inflammations - simply pour onto the compress and place it on the affected eye for 2 - 3 minutes, three times a day.

USE:

HEALTH EFFECTS:

Chamomile has antibacterial and anti-inflammatory properties. The tea can be used to soothe stomach or intestinal difficulties. Compresses or baths soothe inflammations and support the healing process. A steam bath is beneficial for colds and sore throats.

COSMETICS:

To keep your blond hair fair use chamomile regularly (2 ounces of leaves in 1 pint of water, allow to ferment). Drink one cup of tea regularly to cleanse your stomach and your skin.

DECORATIVE USES:

The plant looks great along paths or on the borders of flowerbeds. If you walk along such a path you can smell the intense scent.

IMPORTANT PRECAUTION:

Sensitive people might be allergic to chamomile. Such people should not use chamomile tea on their eyes.

Melissa officinalis
Lemon balm

Type:
∞

Location for growth:

Use:

FAMILY: Labiate family (*Lamiaceae*)

ORIGIN: Lemon balm is also called folia melissae because of its scent. It originated in the Orient and the Mediterranean area. It deserves a permanent place in gardens due to several of its characteristics. It is famous for its use in the production of lemon balm liqueur.

FEATURES: This perennial shrub grows up to 30 inches tall. It has broad shoots and many leaves. The leaves give off an intense lemony scent, especially when you rub them. The white-yellow blossoms, which grow in bunches in summer, attract many bees and butterflies. Lemon balm is rich in essential oils, tannins, and alkaloids.

SPECIAL TIP: "Aurea," with golden yellow leaves, and "Variegata," with golden variagated leaves, are very decorative.

LOCATION FOR GROWTH: Lemon balm grows mainly in sunny places but it can be partially shaded as well. It is better to plant it where it is sheltered from wind. The soil should be rich and loose, and you can cover it with sand.

CULTIVATION: The seedlings are started in boxes in spring and kept at 70°F. You should tend to the plant every day because the seedlings sprout no sooner than 2 - 3 weeks after planting. As soon as the weather is warmer you can plant the seedlings outdoors, or you can save time by planting cuttings. Young plants are available in shops, and they grow quickly. During the growing phase, water frequently and remove parts of the plant if it gets too thick. Alternatively you can plant lemon balm in a pot or balcony planter. The plant should be covered during cold winters.

HARVEST: You can harvest the young leaves and shoots from spring to fall. To get the freshest aroma and the highest content of the valuable substances, use lemon balm when it is fresh. You can cut and dry the plant before it flowers to keep a reserve for the winter.

SPECIAL TIP:

RELAXING AND STRENGTHENING ESSENCE
Mix 7 ounces fresh lemon balm leaves with 1 quart brandy and put in a warm place. Set aside for about 10 days and then filter. Squeeze the leaves dry, so that the essence is properly extracted. Essence of lemon balm is used to strengthen the heart and blood circulation, and it also helps with nervousness and problems with sleeping. Drink it mixed with water or tea.

USE:

CUISINE:
Lemon balm makes all foods taste better where a lemony aroma is needed, for example salads, fish, or soups. You should not cook it; if you do, you lose the spicy taste. To refresh yourself, drink lemon balm tea. It will taste even better if you combine it with dog rose, hibiscus, or orange leaf tea.

HEALTH EFFECTS:
The essential oil of lemon balm is used for calming oneself during stressful situations and helps with sleep problems. The tannins and bitter substances help with stomach ailments. The dried leaves are used for preparing relaxing tea, which is even better if you add 1 teaspoon of honey.

COSMETICS:
Dried leaves are often used as a bath ingredient to promote relaxation. For a bath you need 2 ounces lemon balm leaves, boiled in 1 quart of water. After 10 minutes, when it has cooled down, you can add it to the bath.

DECORATIVE USES:
You will certainly enjoy yellow lemon balm leaves in your flowerbeds.

Mentha x piperita
Peppermint

FAMILY: Labiate family (*Lamiaceae*)

ORIGIN: Peppermint was crossbred from water mint (*Mentha aquatica*) and spearmint (*M. spicata*). This plant, with its intense aroma, has been popular since the end of the 17th century. It is also called tea mint or English mint.

FEATURES: The plant grows to a height of 30 inches. Mint leaves are usually green, though sometimes they change to a reddish color similar to that of the shoot, or to a pinkish violet color in summer. The plant is reproduced from underground shoots. The most important substance in the plant is its essential oil, menthol.

SPECIAL TIP: The 'Mitcham' type, with its blue-green leaves, is probably the most famous of mints. It has a peppermint aroma and grows robustly. 'Citrata' smells like cologne. There are also types with lemony and orange scents.

SIMILAR SPECIES: *Spearmint*, the ancestor of peppermint, is known for its high menthol content and was originally used to flavor chewing gum.

LOCATION FOR GROWTH: Mint needs partial shade with damp, rich soil. It can grow in sunny places if it is not too dry.

CULTIVATION: Peppermint has no seeds, unlike other mint types, and it reproduces only from its root shoots so to begin growing it you need to buy the first plant. Alternatively, ask a neighbor or friend if they have any mint shoots to spare. Mint makes a good ground cover because it grows in thick clumps. The plants usually grow tall, and can be seen with other plants next to them. When blight appears, the plant should be cut back radically. It grows back quickly. Protect the plant against freezing in winter.

HARVEST: You can harvest the leaves all season long. Cut it back before it blooms if you want to dry it. You should do this late in the summer.

SPECIAL TIP:

MINT LIQUEUR

Mix a pound of fresh mint leaves, the juice of 2 oranges, and a pinch of nutmeg with a pint of 96% alcohol, and pour into a glass bottle. The alcohol is available at drugstores. Leave this bottle in a sunny place for 3 weeks and then filter it. Finally, warm it gently with 20 ounces of sugar and 1 quart water. Pour the liqueur into small, decorative bottles and set it aside for a couple of weeks before you drink it or give it as presents.

USE:

CUISINE:

The fresh leaves are used in herbal salads, sauces, soups, and vegetable or meat dishes. You can use it as a garnish that can be eaten. Fresh and dried leaves are used for preparing tea.

HEALTH EFFECTS:

The menthol contained in peppermint has calming effects and is good for relieving cramps. Peppermint tea soothes discomfort caused by digestive problems, and inhalations are used to get rid of a cold and stuffy nose.

COSMETICS:

Peppermint leaves in a bath are refreshing, and good for skin pores. You can make peppermint body oil by mixing 1 handful fresh leaves with a pint of olive or almond oil. Allow to sit for 1 week.

USE FOR DECORATION:

The scent of peppermint is pleasant and attracts many bees and butterflies.

IMPORTANT PRECAUTION:

You should avoid using peppermint if you have serious stomach problems. Some people are allergic to menthol. It would be better to choose fennel tea for small children suffering from stomach aches because peppermint's high menthol content can cause breathing problems.

Mentha suaveolens
Apple mint

Type:

∞

Location for growth:

☀ – ☀

Use:

✕ 🐜 🏆 ❀

Features:

!

FAMILY: Labiate plants (*Lamiaceae*)

ORIGIN: This round-leafed mint originated in eastern and southern Europe and spread from the British Isles to southern Sweden. It is popular as a culinary and decorative herb, and is found in many places growing wild.

FEATURES: This plant grows quickly from its roots in the garden, reaching a height of 3 feet or more. It has many fruit-scented leaves, which is why the English call it apple mint. It flowers with white or pink flowers in late summer.

SPECIAL TIP: The 'Variegata' type has gray-green leaves and is also called pineapple mint because it has creamy white spots and smells of pineapple. It is quite robust and resistant to cold, and it is used as a decorative plant.

SIMILAR SPECIES: Another apple-scented mint (*Mentha* x *rotundifolia*) is a cross of Ross mint (*M.longifolia*) and round-leafed mint. It has silvery leaves and pink-lilac flowers. The 'Bowles' type is famous for its fruity scent.

LOCATION FOR GROWTH: Apple mint needs light shade and damp, rich soil, as do other mints. It can grow in the sun but does not like dryness.

CULTIVATION: It is best to buy young plants in spring and plant in rich, damp soil. To shape a broad shrub, prune it repeatedly. Mint grows into shrubs and nicely covers ground in your garden. It usually grows tall when you water it frequently. It is enough to fertilize the ground in spring. If it is not growing well, cut it back. Cut it back when the plant is covered with blight. It grows back quickly. Protect the plant in colder areas.

HARVEST: You can harvest fresh leaves all summer. Cut it back before it blooms if you want to dry it. You should repeat the process, best in late summer.

SPECIAL TIP:

TRADITIONAL ENGLISH MINT SAUCE

You need approximately 8 tablespoons mint leaves. Chop them fine and pour 4 tablespoons boiling water over them. Then add 1 tablespoon honey and set aside for 1 hour. Add 3 tablespoons balsamic or wine vinegar shortly before serving and stir well. Mint sauce is delicious and is often served with lamb.

USE:

CUISINE:
The fresh, fruity flavor goes well with sweet dishes and makes a tasty tea. The leaves must be cooked because of the hairs.

HEALTH EFFECTS:
Apple mint contains menthol like peppermint does, and is used for stomach and intestinal problems. Inhaling helps with colds or the flu.

Apple mint

COSMETICS:
The leaves are used as a bath ingredient or in cleansing enemas.

DECORATIVE USES:
Apple mint is a decorative, scented plant that is popular in gardens. It decorates the sides of paths with its green color. It is also planted to adorn balconies and hanging pots.

IMPORTANT PRECAUTION:

This plant does not contain as much menthol as peppermint, but the amount it does contain can cause adverse reactions too.

Monarda didyma
Scarlet Bee-Balm

Type:

Location for growth:
☼ – ☀

Use:
✗ ♣ ✿

FAMILY: Labiate family (*Lamiaceae*)

ORIGIN: Native North Americans used Scarlet Bee-Balm as a therapeutic plant, hence it is also called "Indian nettle." After the discovery of America, it was spread across Europe. There are many variants of this plant, due to cross-breeding, which no longer have any therapentic benefits.

FEATURES: The plant grows as a shrub and reaches heights of 30 - 60 inches depending on the type and richness of the soil. It grows fast because of its flat, thick root system, and it forms dense bushes. The leaves are long and grow opposite each other. Red blossoms appear all over the richly-scented plant in late summer.

SPECIAL TIP: 'Marshall's Delight' blooms are pink, and it can be used as wild art. 'Adam' and 'Garden View Scarlet' have red blooms, 'Beauty of Cobham' is violet pink, 'Croftway Pink' is salmon pink, and 'Schneewittchen' is innocent white.

SIMILAR SPECIES: *Monarda fistulosa*, which originated in sunny California and Mexico, has an aroma similar to that of

thyme. Its blooms are lilac in color. *M. punctata* has yellow spotted blossoms. The leaves smell a bit like oregano.

LOCATION FOR GROWTH: Scarlet bee-balm calls for simple conditions. It needs a sunny place with damp soil; it can also grow in partial shade and drier places. It is essential to protect it from direct sun at noon.

CULTIVATION: You can get the wild form of scarlet bee-balm as a seedling or plant at specialized herb gardens. Once it is sown in a garden it grows by itself without any effort. You can cut it back in spring, collect the roots, or take cuttings.

It can spread more than 12 - 15 inches if you give it enough space. The ground should be fertilized each year in the spring. The plant should be cut back to just above the ground for the winter. It is good to cut it back and separate it every two years to rejuvenate it.

Harvest: You can harvest the fresh leaves from spring until fall and gather the blossoms; the summertime is the best period for this. Cut the plant back before it blooms if you want to dry it for tea in the winter.

Special tip:

Homemade lemonade
Gather some blossom tops and pour a pint of boiling water over them. Let cool and then put it in the refridgerator. Add the juice of 1 - 2 squeezed lemons, sweeten to taste and top off with sparkling mineral water. You can use mint, lemon balm, or Mexican mint as alternative herbs.

USE:

CUISINE:

The leaves are used to make a refreshing tea that helps stimulate digestion. You can add it as flavoring to other teas to make different tea variations. You can prepare your own special Earl Grey tea by adding scarlet bee-balm leaves to black tea. Salads can also be garnished with the leaves.

HEALTH EFFECTS:

Drink the tea for colds, the flu, or simply to relax! To prepare a tea mixture, gather leaves and blossoms together.

DECORATIVE USES:

Aromatic scarlet bee-balm looks great in herb gardens and flowerbeds. It also grows well in light shade, and attracts bees and butterflies. Good neighbors for this plant are clove, caryopsis, elecampane, and goldenrod. The scented leaves are often used to produce potpourri.

Myrrhis odorata
Sweet cicely

Type:
∞

Location for growth:

Use:

FAMILY: Carrot family (*Apiaceae*)

ORIGIN: Sweet cicely is native to damp forests and mountains from southern Europe to the Caucasus. It is a relative of chervil, so it is also called sweet chervil or Spanish chervil. Its leaves were used as dyes - green or orange-brown. We should copy the Scandinavians and keep this aromatic plant - which keeps for a long time and is winter-hardy - in our gardens.

FEATURES: You can mistake this plant's pretty green leaves for a fern when it is not blooming. But when you come closer to it, you will smell the anise scent which comes from the essential oil anethol. In late spring and early summer, flat white flowers appear, followed by delicious fruits, which also have an anise or licorice flavor. It grows up to 5 feet tall.

SIMILAR SPECIES: Do not mistake sweet cicely for licorice, (*Glycyrrhiza glabra*) the roots of which are used in licorice candy. Take licorice in small amounts to help against stomach and digestion problems. Licorice tea made from the roots helps with stomach, phlegm, and skin problems, but when

used too often or in large amounts it can cause high blood pressure.

LOCATION FOR GROWTH: Sweet cicely is easy to grow almost anywhere, in shade or full sun. The soil should be rich and moist.

CULTIVATION: You can sow the seeds in fall or late winter. Overgrown plants can be cut back and will regrow in spring. Once it has been started, sweet cicely reseeds itself. This can be avoided by cutting off the blossom shoots. Use mulch to keep the ground damp. After blooming the plant should be cut back.

HARVEST: You can harvest the plant regularly, as young leaves and shoots are especially smooth. It is most aromatic when it is fresh, but you can also freeze the leaves for later use. The fruit tastes best when it is green and not yet ripe. You can use the roots as a vegetable in dishes if you dig them up in the fall.

SPECIAL TIP:

SWEETS FROM THE GARDEN
Children like cicely fruits. They taste best when still fresh off the plant and have a sweet, pleasant flavor.

USE:

CUISINE:

You can make salads, soups, and sauces taste better by adding the leaves of this plant. You need just a small piece of leaf to flavor food with a sweet anise taste. Cook rhubarb or other stewed fruit together with sweet cicely leaves and they will be even better. The shoots are especially suitable for stewing. You can eat the fresh green fruits alone or add them to fruit salads and cereals. Sweet cicely is a good substitute for anise, fennel, or licorice.

HEALTH EFFECTS:

Sweet cicely helps with digestive problems and is a mild laxative. It cures coughs and strengthens against anemia.

DECORATIVE USES:

Sweet cicely is a very unusual and special plant for shady places, and is covered with white blossoms. It is full of nectar and many insects enjoy it. If you are skilful you can decorate writing paper with the shapes of the pressed leaves.

Myrtus communis
Myrtle

Type:

⊙

Location for growth:

☼ – ☀

Use:

FAMILY: Myrtle plants (*Myrtaceae*)

ORIGIN: Myrtle is associated with the Mediterranean region, but you can also find it from central Asia to northern Africa. The ancient Greeks saw it as symbol of beauty and love. The shoots were used as decoration during feasts and brides were adorned with myrtle wreaths too. That is why this plant is sometimes called 'Bride-myrtle.'

FEATURES: This evergreen can grow up to 16 feet, but it is usually planted in pots, where it does not grow so tall. Leaves with oil glands are typical for this plant. The scented white blossoms appear at the end of spring and ripen to black berries. The plant contains a great deal of essential oil as well as resins, tannins, and alkaloids.

SPECIAL TIP: With its yellow leaves, the 'Variegata' type is very decorative.

SIMILAR SPECIES: Another member of the myrtle family is the tea tree (*Melaleuca*). Even though other plants of this family can be planted in pots, usually only myrtle is available to

buy. However, this may change as the tea tree is now coming into vogue because of its healing effects.

LOCATION FOR GROWTH: Myrtle likes sunny places but can also grow in light shade. The soil should be free of clay.

CULTIVATION: It should not be difficult to find this plant at garden centers. It does not like clay and should be frequently watered with rainwater or soft water. During the growing period rhododendron fertilizer can be used. Myrtle can be damaged from frequent cutting - the best time is in spring, when cuttings take root most easily. It can stand short frost periods but, it is always better to take it inside the house and put it in good light at 104 - 122°F to hibernate.

HARVEST: Myrtle leaves can be picked all year, so you can always use them fresh.

SPECIAL TIP:

THE FIRST BITE IS WITH THE EYE!
Garnish fresh salads with pretty, aromatic flowers and buds. Remove the leaves before serving.

USE:

CUISINE:

Myrtle is used much like rosemary or thyme for grilling meat. The leaves can be ground like bay laurel. The berries can be cooked in sauces.

HEALTH EFFECTS:

The leaves contain an essential oil with antiseptic effects, which also helps with breathing problems. Myrtle tea works well against bronchial infections and gum inflammations. The crushed leaves help with skin problems such as acne, dandruff, and herpes.

COSMETICS:

Myrtle is a base ingredient for perfumes and cosmetic products. The dried leaves and flowers give off a pleasant scent that persists for a long time and makes them useful for sachets or potpourris.

DECORATIVE USES:

Myrtle is aromatic all year round. You can plant it in pots to enjoy all summer, or if you have a winter garden you can enjoy the scent and feeling of a Mediterranean summer all winter.

Nasturtium officinale
Watercress

FAMILY: Mustard family (*Brassicaceae*)

ORIGIN: Originally watercress came from Europe, but now you can find it in every temperate area. It usually grows around water and is sometimes called water or brook nasturtium. The Romans used it when preparing salads and seasoning foods. You can find it under the name *"Rorippa nasturtium-aquaticum."*

FEATURES: This water and marsh plant grows up to 30 inches tall with dense leaves. Thick roots hold the plant firmly in place and the leaves hang above and under the water. In the summer, the white flowers contrast nicely with the dark green shoots. The leaves contain a bitter essential oil (mustard oil glucoside), vitamins, mineral substances, tannins and alkaloids.

SIMILAR SPECIES: Small-leafed watercress (*Nasturtium microphyllum*) is known for its frost resistance.

LOCATION FOR GROWTH: Watercress is a salad herb that can grow in colder places in partial or full shade. It prefers rich clay soil, which must always be damp.

CULTIVATION: The plants need your attention while growing because they need water that is 3 feet deep. You can find such conditions in marshy areas around small lakes.

HARVEST: The best parts to eat are the new leaves and shoots, which should be harvested before the flowers come. Store them in a glass of water in a shaded area to keep them fresh. It is very important to wash them before use.

SPECIAL TIP:

WATERCRESS SALAD WITH AVOCADO

To make a green salad you need 1 - 2 handfuls watercress and some dandelion, nettle, and birch leaves. Slice one avocado and gently lay it in the salad. Cover with a vinaigrette dressing and the juice of a squeezed lemon. Add salt and pepper. This mixture, which is rich in vitamins, is good all year round.

USE

CUISINE:

You can use watercress together with other greens. It also tastes good in sandwiches or in herbal cottage cheese. It adds zing to soups, as well!

HEALTH EFFECTS:

This herb stimulates the gall bladder, kidneys, and liver. It stimulates digestion and purifies the blood, and in spring you can use it for dieting. It helps with rheumatism and gout.

COSMETICS:

Watercress juice contains an antibiotic essential oil that clears and purifies the skin. Use a swab to apply it to irritated places. You can also lighten summer freckles by applying the crushed herb to your skin at night.

DECORATIVE USES:

Watercress is grown on the banks of garden ponds or brooks and covers them with its white flowers.

IMPORTANT PRECAUTION:

When gathering watercress in the wild, be aware of the cleanliness of the water in which the plant is growing, otherwise you may be at risk from water-borne diseases and parasites. You can irritate your kidneys by overdosing on watercress, so eat no more than an ounce per day.

Nepeta cataria
Catnip

FAMILY: Labiate family (*Lamiaceae*)

ORIGIN: Catnip (also called catmint) originated in Europe. It also grows in central Asia and the Himalayas. It is planted in many gardens as a therapeutic plant with a pleasant scent and a calming effect. It was used as a natural dye in the past.

FEATURES: Catnip can grow to 12 - 40 inches tall depending on where it is grown. The leaves look like nettles at first glance, but in summer you can see the real beauty of this plant, with its purple and white flowers. The leaves smell like lemon and mint, and the plant is a stimulant for cats.

SPECIAL TIP: 'Citriodora,' or white lemon balm, is a traditional garden plant. It has a nice lemony aroma and is used for making tea. The leaves have a nice scent even after drying, and are sometimes darker than catnip leaves. It grows well in the shade and harder soil.

SIMILAR SPECIES: Blue catmint (*Nepeta* x *faassenii*) has an almost magical effect on cats. It grows well in sunny places

and dry rock gardens. The leaves are gray-green. "Six Hills Giant" has lavender-colored flowers, and "Snowflakes" has white ones. Cut it back after the first bloom and it grows back before fall. It looks good in flowerbeds along with roses and other plants.

LOCATION FOR GROWTH: Catnip grows in sun as well as in partial-shade; it prefers damp clay-rich soil.

CULTIVATION: You can buy a young plant or shoot to start. It may grow for only 3 – 4 years but this is not so bad since it reseeds itself if grown in a suitable place. You can plant cuttings in the spring or fall.

HARVEST: You can harvest the fresh leaves all summer. They dry easily, so you can use them for tea in winter.

SPECIAL TIP:

CATS LOVE IT!
Catnip has intoxicant effects on cats when they eat or smell it. Other good plants for cats are muscatel, cat-gamander, and valerian.

Use:

Cuisine:

You can make a refreshing, relaxing herbal tea from the leaves of the plant. It tastes good when used sparingly in salads.

Health effects:

Catnip works against cramps and helps with digestion and flatulence, as well as fever and sweating. It is useful for colds and the flu. Diluted, the tea can be given to children and infants. If you suffer from sleep problems or stress, drink catnip tea.

Decorative uses:

Catnip's aroma attracts bees. All catnip plants are very decorative; the types that do not grow very tall look great bordering flowerbeds and garden paths.

Ocimum basilicum
Basil

Type:

Location for growth:

Use:

FAMILY: *Lamiaceae*

ORIGIN: Basil has been a popular herb in Asia for many centuries. Today it grows in Europe in many varieties and types.

FEATURES: This plant grows up to 20 inches tall, depending on the climate and environment. It has thick, long, round leaves, rich in essential oils. If you do not pick it regularly, the plant develops white to pink flowers in the summer. Basil grows in many variations and types, which differ in flavor, leaf color, and shape.

SPECIAL TIP: You can now not only buy basil variants with big or small leaves and red to purple flowers, but also exciting colors such as "Ararat," "Dark Opal," or "Purple Delight." Pink-blooming "Siam Queen" is suitable for terraces and balconies. With regard to scent, you can choose from lemon basil, cinnamon basil, anise basil, spicy Thai basil or exotic Mexican basil.

SIMILAR SPECIES: Small basil (*Ocimum tenuiflorum*) has small, sharp leaves with a good taste.

LOCATION FOR GROWTH: Basil needs a warm, sunny place with rich, damp soil in order to develop its full aroma.

CULTIVATION: This plant, which needs warmth to grow, is usually germinated indoors in the spring at 60 - 70°F. The seeds should only be lightly covered with soil. Seed boxes or pots should be kept in a warm place near a window, and you can put the plant outside when there is no longer danger of frost. The soil should be well tilled. Basil grows well on windowed porches, but will die if you do not water it properly.

HARVEST: The young leaves can be picked all year if you take basil inside for winter. You can dry or freeze the leaves for later use, but they lose their aroma. They should be picked before the flowers blossom.

SPECIAL TIP:

CLASSIC PESTO

2 handfuls basil leaves should be washed and dried, and the thick stems removed.

Stir with 1 teaspoon pine nuts, 1 pressed garlic clove and approximately 3 tablespoons olive oil. Add salt and pepper to taste. The sauce tastes good with pasta, served along with Parmesan cheese.

USE:

CUISINE:
Basil is used very often in Mediterranean cuisine. It goes well with salads and pasta dishes and also in meat or fish dishes. It makes heavy meals more digestible.

HEALTH EFFECTS:
The essential oil calms nerves and relieves stress. Basil leaf tea helps with stomach cramps and stimulates your appetite.

COSMETICS:
Basil is very useful for keeping your breath fresh. Add 1 handful fresh leaves to 1 cup hot water, steep for 15 minutes and rinse your mouth with it.

DECORATIVE USES:
With its variety and different scents, basil looks great on balconies and terraces. The flowers also attract bees and butterflies.

Oenothera biennis
Evening Primrose

Type:

∞

Location for growth:

Use:

FAMILY: Evening primrose (*Onagraceae*)

ORIGIN: This plant grows broadly from northern America to Mexico, but can also be found in Europe; it grows alongside paths or other places with sandy subsoil. Its roots are used as a delicious vegetable, and a therapeutic oil is extracted from the seeds.

FEATURES: This biennial is also known as Onagra biennis. The first year, the roots and leaf rosettes develop, then during the second year the stalk grows up to 7 feet tall, with light yellow flowers. A special feature of this plant is that the sweet, lemon-scented flowers open only at nightfall - in the morning they close again and wilt. The evening primrose is rich in gamma-linoleic acid (GLA), which is an essential fatty acid.

SIMILAR SPECIES: Missouri evening primrose (*Oenothera macrocarpa*, syn. *O. missouriensis*) grows to only 8 inches in height. Its yellow flowers appear all summer, releasing a lemony aroma in the evenings and attracting butterflies.

LOCATION FOR GROWTH: The plant needs to be in full sun to partial shade. It grows almost anywhere and prefers sandy soil.

CULTIVATION: If you want to harvest the large, thick roots, start it indoors from April to May. The strong seedlings should be then planted, spaced 8 - 10 inches apart. You can sow it outdoors from June to August, in rows spaced 8 inches apart and then later thin the seedlings to a spacing of 8 - 10 inches. The plant does not need any special care until you harvest its roots in the fall. It does not need especially rich soil and it reseeds itself.

HARVEST: The roots can be harvested from fall until spring. You can store them in a cool cellar. The roots should be harvested before flowering; otherwise they will not be useful.

SPECIAL TIP:

AN INVIGORATING ROOT VEGETABLE
Dig up the thick roots in fall and clean them well. Cook with vinegar and oil or in a broth. This old household remedy helped patients recover from illness.

EVENING PRIMROSE OIL BATH FOR DRY SKIN
Heat 1 cup cream or 2 cups milk, add 2 tablespoons honey and 20 drops of evening primrose oil, and stir well. Add to your bath.

USE:

CUISINE:

The roots should be cleaned and cooked, or you can chop them and add them to salads raw.

HEALTH EFFECTS:

The oil is used for many reasons. It is mostly taken internally as drops or in capsules. Arthritis and premenstrual problems are treated with it, as well as high blood pressure. You can prepare tea from the tops of the blossoms, which will be helpful for relieving coughs and digestive problems.

COSMETICS:

The oil softens brittle nails and dry skin. It is effective against acne and eczema. Use it in your bath!

DECORATIVE USES:

The plant looks great in rock gardens, and it can be planted in pots. It attracts bees and butterflies, and gives off a lovely scent in the evenings.

Origanum majorana
Marjoram

Type:

Location for growth:

Use:

Features:

FAMILY: Labiate family (*Lamiaceae*)

ORIGIN: Thanks to the Arabian peoples, this spice plant still grows in the Mediterranean area, where it originated. It was famous among the Romans and Greeks for its many beneficial properties. It was added to rich red wines as an aphrodisiac.

FEATURES: In its area of origin the plant is a perennial, but it is an annual in colder climates. It has red shoots up to 20 inches tall and gray aromatic leaves. In summer the flowers are white, pink, or lavender. It is rich in essential oils, tannins and bitter substances.

SIMILAR SPECIES: *Origanum* x *majoricum* is a cross of oregano and marjoram, and it tastes like a mixture of the two. The plant is bigger and more robust than marjoram, and is also an annual. It propagates through its seeds; you should cut the plant back in late summer.

LOCATION FOR GROWTH: Marjoram needs the same conditions as oregano: sun, warmth and moist soil.

CULTIVATION: You can buy young marjoram plants at any garden shop. Plant marjoram seed early indoors or in the garden in May, once the ground is warm. The seeds should be only lightly covered with soil. Space the seedlings 2 - 3 inches apart. Marjoram grows well in tilled soil. Do not cut it too far back when harvesting, or else it cannot grow back.

HARVEST: You can gather the leaves and flowers throughout summer and use them fresh. If you want to dry it, cut it right

before or during its blooming period. You can also preserve
it in oil.

SPECIAL TIP:

CRISPY POTATOES WITH MARJORAM

**Use small potatoes, which cook more quickly. Cut them into
halves and lay them flat side down on an oiled baking sheet.
Bake in the bottom level of an oven pre-heated to 400°F for
about 30 minutes. For a delicious crispy crust, you need 1 –
2 bunches of marjoram - washed, dried, and chopped. Mix
three-quarters of the marjoram with 2 ounces chopped sunflower seeds and 1 teaspoon black caraway seeds, adding salt
and pepper. Cover the potatoes with the mixture and drizzle
with oil. Bake 5 - 10 minutes, using the rest of the marjoram to
garnish the dish before serving.**

USE:

CUISINE:

The aroma is well suited to soups, potatoes, and meat dishes. It is often used as a pizza flavoring and in the production of sausages.

HEALTH EFFECTS:

Marjoram contains substances that aid digestion and make heavy foods taste lighter. Marjoram tea strengthens your nerves and stomach, stimulates your appetite and eases cramps. The ancient Egyptians used this plant for disinfecting wounds.

IMPORTANT PRECAUTION:

Like oregano, marjoram contains essential oil, tannins, and bitter alkaloids. Regular ingestion can cause headaches and dizziness. It is used to support the female libido in homeopathy. Therefore pregnant women should avoid taking it internally.

DECORATIVE USES:

Marjoram grows as an annual on balconies or in pots. It smells good in dried potpourris.

Origanum vulgare
Oregano

Type:

⊙

Location for growth:

☼

Use:

✗ ♉ ⚘

Features:

!

FAMILY: Labiate family (*Lamiaceae*)

ORIGIN: Oregano, or wild marjoram, originated in southern Europe and subsequently spread to Scandinavia as well as to Central and North America.

FEATURES: This shrub can grow up to 20 inches tall. It has thick roots and grows easily. Its flowers are pinkish-violet and appear in umbels. The plant contains not only tannins and alkaloids, but also an essential oil containing thymol. A powerful scent is released when you crush the leaves.

SPECIAL TIPS: "Album" has white flowers and grows to only 12 inches in height. "Aureum" has yellow leaves and requires partial shade. "Compactum" grows to only 8 inches and makes an excellent ground cover.

LOCATION FOR GROWTH: Oregano develops its full aroma only when it is grown in a warm, sunny, dry place. The ground should be sandy, rich and moist.

CULTIVATION: One or two plants are sufficient for household use. You can germinate oregano seed indoors in early spring and plant the seedlings outside later. Do not plant them too close to each other; the best spacing is 8 to 10 inches apart. Cover the plants with mulch in colder winters, and then prune well in the spring so that new shoots can grow.

HARVEST: You can gather the young leaves and tops for drying in fall, or use them fresh. For the best dried oregano, harvest it before it blooms, as the aroma is strongest then. The plant is aromatic even when dried. Alternatively, you can preserve it in oil.

Special tip:

Quick tomato soup
Sauté 1 small onion and 1 pressed garlic clove in a little butter and add half a cup of vegetable broth, together with 4 peeled tomatoes, 1 teaspoon of oregano, and crushed thyme to taste. Cook for 10 minutes, and just before serving pour cream on top and add salt. You might want to use some basil leaves to garnish the soup.

Use:

Cuisine:
This classic pizza herb, with its bitter aromatic taste, is also good in soups, meats, and pasta. It is mixed with other herbs to produce the famous blend 'Herbes de Provence.'

Health effects:
The bitter substances affect gall-bladder function. Tea made from 1 spoonful of the herb steeped in 1 cup boiling water soothes stomach and intestinal problems such as diarrhea. Oregano tea can relieve a troublesome cough if you add honey.

Cosmetics:
The essential oil that oregano contains is used in many cosmetic products.

Decorative uses:
Oregano is a beautiful herb, and it attracts bees, butterflies, and many other insects. It looks great in rock gardens or in the upper levels of an herbal spiral. It grows well on balconies and in pots. The dried blossoms look great in bouquets of dried plants.

Important precaution:

Pregnant women should use oregano tea carefully, as it strongly stimulates the stomach and pancreas, and also contains a potent essential oil. It can irritate sensitive skin.

Petroselinum crispum
Parsley

Type:

∞ – ⊙

Location for growth:

☼ – ☀

Use:

Features:

!

FAMILY: Carrot family (*Apiaceae*)

ORIGIN: This herb originated in southern Europe, and was used medicinally by the ancient Greeks and Romans. It was forgotten for a long time, but returned to the kitchen in the 15th century.

FEATURES: Parsley is a biennial herb. In the first year, roots and leaf rosettes form, and then the next summer it produces yellowish-green flowers and reaches a height of 25 inches. Once the seeds develop only a few leaves continue to grow. The roots and leaves contain large amounts of vitamin C, as well as important minerals such as calcium and iron and essential oils. The seeds are especially rich in parsley camphor.

SPECIAL TIPS: Parsley has lush, flat leaves, and the leaves at the tips have a stronger flavor. Famous curly-leaved types include "Green Pearle" and "Emerald." "Green River" has sturdy, curly leaves and is very hardy. The renowned "Gigante d'Italia" has flat leaves and a very fine flavor.

SIMILAR SPECIES: Root parsley (*Petroselinum crispum* var. *tuberosum*) has richly-flavored roots as well as green herbal leaves.

LOCATION FOR GROWTH: This plant needs full sun to partial shade. The soil should be rich, deep and moist for the plant to grow well.

CULTIVATION: You can plant leaf parsley seeds starting in the middle of March, spaced 6 - 8 inches apart. If you sow new seeds regularly you can harvest leaves from the plant throughout its growing season. If you are planting root parsley, wait about 4 weeks until the ground is warmer. The seeds will germinate and grow more quickly if you mix them with radish seeds, so you can watch your parsley progress! Seeds and plants need to be in damp soil, though not excessively wet. Late-sown parsley stays green in the winter if well covered. You can also cultivate parsley in pots on windowsills.

Harvest: You can harvest fresh leaves, and they can be preserved by freezing. The roots should be dug up in late fall and put in sand for storage in a cool cellar. Alternatively you can freeze or dry the roots.

Special tip:

Cleansing, purifying face wash
Boil 2 tablespoons crushed parsley in 1 cup of peppermint tea, cover, and set aside for 30 minutes. Apply to the skin.

USE

CUISINE:

Parsley is used to season soups, sauces, and egg dishes, potatoes, vegetable dishes and salads. Herb-enriched cottage cheese and parsley butter are also tasty. Add the parsley just before serving, because it loses its vitamins when cooked. The roots can be added to soups and stews.

HEALTH EFFECTS:

Parsley is rich in vitamin C. It purifies your blood and supports blood cell production.

COSMETICS:

Parsley oil is used in perfumes. A fresh mash of parsley soothes inflammations and cleanses the skin.

DECORATIVE USES:

Curly-leafed parsley looks especially great on balconies and terraces when planted in pots.

Peterseliewortel

IMPORTANT PRECAUTION:

Parsley oil can cause kidney and liver problems. It can cause abortion; so pregnant women should not use it. There is only a small amount of parsley oil in the leaves and roots.

Pimpinella anisum
Anise

FAMILY: Carrot family (*Apiaceae*)

ORIGIN: Anise was a popular spice in the Mediterranean as early as 3,000 years ago. It spread quickly throughout the Mediterranean countries and was brought to northern Europe by monks. Anise is now grown mainly in sunny, southern Europe.

FEATURES: This annual can grow up to 20 – 28 inches tall. Its three different leaf forms - all on the same plant - are worth noting. The lower leaves are round, the central leaves are indented with three folds, and the upper leaves are thin and deeply scalloped. The stems grow from the leaf rosettes, and branch out near their tops. In late summer the plant produces white umbels from which brown, sweet-tasting fruits mature, each one consisting of two separate parts. The fruits (aniseeds) contain a large amount of an essential oil called anethol, as well as fatty acids, albumen, and sugar.

SIMILAR SPECIES: The Greater Burnet Saxifrage (*Pimpinella major*) grows widely along roadsides in northern latitudes. A tea made from its dried roots helps against bronchial infec-

tions and swelling of the throat. Both its roots and anise roots are used in homoeopathic preparations.

LOCATION FOR GROWTH: Because fruits ripen fully only when grown in warm, sunny places, the anise harvest cannot take place during cold, wet summers. The ideal soil should contain humus and calcium, and should have good drainage.

CULTIVATION: Anise can be sown directly in beds starting in April. However, starting the seeds indoors is recommended, as they germinate faster that way. The seeds must be properly covered with soil, and it can be weeks before the dark sprouts emerge. The seedlings should be planted later, spaced 10 inches apart. The soil should be well tilled and without weeds. This is especially important for the first planting.

HARVEST: Harvest the aniseeds as soon as the seeds turn brown, either cutting off the mature seed heads or the whole plant. The seeds should be spread over a piece of linen and left to dry; they can then be stored for some time without losing their aroma. Fresh anise leaves can be harvested throughout the summer.

A SPECIAL TIP:

ANISE NESTS

Beat 3 eggs and half a pound sugar until foamy, then add half a pound flour, 1 pinch salt, and 1 teaspoon aniseed powder. Using two teaspoons, place small mounds of dough on a cookie sheet greased with shortening or covered with baking paper. Let sit overnight in a warm place and then bake in an open oven for about 30 minutes at 300 – 320°F.

USE:

CUISINE:

Anise is used in bread and pastry, which is why it is also called "bread seed" in some regions. It is also used as a spice for sweet dishes like fruit salads, and to flavor many Christmas treats. It lends a sweet flavor to soups, sauces, and boiled root vegetables. Anise brandy is wonderful - the aroma is especially strong if the seeds have been ground or crushed before use. Fresh leaves can be added to salads and soups. The intense aroma also ensures fresh breath for those who use it.

HEALTH EFFECTS:

This spice boosts gall-bladder function and improves digestion, making heavy dishes easily digestible - which is why it is a custom in the Orient to chew anise seeds after a meal. Anise is also a popular cure for coughs because it releases phlegm and calms the cough reflex. It also stimulates milk flow in nursing mothers.

DECORATIVE USES:

The plentiful flower umbels are beautiful in herb gardens during the summer.

Portulaca oleracea
Purslane

Type:
∞

Location for growth:
☼

Use:
 𝔄

FAMILY: Purslane family (*Portulacaceae*)

ORIGIN: Purslane probably originated in India, however it was domesticated in the Mediterranean region long ago. Some centuries ago it spread to northern and central Europe, where it is also known as moss rose. At one time it was used to prevent scurvy due to its high vitamin C content.

FEATURES: Summer or vegetable purslane is an annual with red, heavily branched stalks that can grow up to 6 – 12 inches tall, depending on its location. The stalks are round, and the oval leaves are juicy and fleshy. Small yellow flowers appear among the leaves during the summer. Purslane contains a lot of vitamins and essential oils.

TIP FOR SPECIES: As well as the green-leafed purslane, there are also types with broad, yellow leaves.

SIMILAR SPECIES: Miner's lettuce (*Montia perfoliata*) is harvested like spinach shortly before blooming. It tastes good as a green or as a stewed vegetable, as does pink purslane

(*M. sibirica*). The latter grows well in shady places under fruit trees.

LOCATION FOR GROWTH: The ideal spot is a sunny bed protected from wind, with well-tilled, sandy soil.

CULTIVATION: Purslane requires a very warm environment, so it cannot be sown outdoors until May. This sowing can be repeated every three weeks until the beginning of September. Purslane should be sown in rows spaced 8 inches apart, with the seeds loosely spread and covered with only a little soil. Regular watering is important so that the fleshy leaves can grow to their fullest extent. The soil should be well weeded.

HARVEST: Most of the young, juicy leaves can be harvested three or four weeks after sowing. After flowering, however, they taste bitter. Purslane cannot be stored, but you can try to grow them on a window ledge in the winter.

A SPECIAL TIP:

PURSLANE SALAD WITH ASPARAGUS

Cook 2 pounds asparagus in 1 ounce butter, a pinch sugar and 3 tablespoonfuls water for about 10 minutes. Wash and clean half a pound sugar peas and then cook together with the asparagus for 1–2 minutes. While the vegetables are cooling, wash and dry 4 ounces purslane and chop 1 ounce walnuts. Now make a sauce from 2 tablespoonfuls fruit vinegar, 2 teaspoons apple juice and 5 tablespoonfuls walnut oil and add it to the herbs. Toss with the asparagus tops and sugar peas. Garnish with the chopped walnuts.

USE:

CUISINE:

Purslane is added to salads, soups, or sauces. It can also be boiled like spinach. It has an herbal, salty taste. If you find it too bitter, blanch it in boiling water shortly before serving.

HEALTH EFFECTS:

This herb relieves gastric pains and heartburn. Tea made from purslane is calming. Thanks to its blood-cleansing effects, purslane is an ideal ingredient in detox diets. Patients with high cholesterol should eat it regularly.

Rheum rhabarbarum
Rhubarb

FAMILY: Buckwheat family (*Polygonaceae*)

ORIGIN: The original form of rhubarb came from eastern Asia. Since then, this delicious, vitamin-rich plant has become a steady presence in our vegetables gardens.

FEATURES: Common rhubarb is a perennial shrub that survives winters thanks to its thick, fleshy roots. It grows back every spring with large, crinkly leaves. The stalks can be green or red, and grow up to 35 inches tall. In May the plant has whitish-yellow flowers. Rhubarb stalks contain a lot of vitamins and minerals, especially vitamin C and iron. Ascorbic acid gives the plant its typical taste. The leaves are not suitable for ingestion because they contain various toxins.

TIP FOR SPECIES: "Holsteiner Blut" and "Vierländer" have red fleshy stalks, while "The Sutton" has green fleshy stalks.

SIMILAR SPECIES: Extracts from rhubarb roots and rhubarb teas, or Turkish medicinal rhubarb (*Rheum palmatum*) roots have a laxative effect and help with gastric and intestinal

swelling. The decorative "Tanguticum" type is striking, with its large, red blossoms.

LOCATION FOR GROWTH: Rhubarb should be grown in full sun or partial shade. In full shade its stalks are weak. Since rhubarb requires a lot of nutrients and has long roots, the soil should be deep and loose and be rich in humus and nutrients. A rhubarb plant may stay in one place for up to 10 years.

CULTIVATION: Rhubarb seeds are available, but growing rhubarb from seed is time-consuming. You can purchase roots at your garden center and plant them in fall or spring. Make sure that the protrusions stay well under the soil and the stalks are perpendicular to the earth. You could also ask your neighbors if they have an older plant that can be divided! Give the plant lots of space, at least 9 square feet. Rhubarb must always be watered well, and the flowers should be cut off immediately. The harvest can be hastened if you cover the plant with plastic, fleece or boxes in late winter.

HARVEST: The thick stalks can be harvested up to the end of June. Do not cut them off; you should pick them by twisting. Leave some stalks so the plant can grow back. Strip the skin off and eat the stalks raw or boiled.

A SPECIAL TIP:

RHUBARB DESSERT
Stew one pound chopped rhubarb with a quarter-pound of sugar, 1 lemon peel and 1 cup water. Beat 2 ounces cornstarch with 2 egg yolks and 1 cup cider or apple juice. Ladle the fruit into bowls and top with the apple froth. Serve with vanilla sauce or cream.

USE:

CUISINE:

The stalks may be used for compote, marmalade, pie or juice. They are a sour but tasty ingredient; the acidity can be balanced by adding nuts.

HEALTH EFFECTS:

Rhubarb has a high vitamin and mineral content. Turkish medicinal rhubarb has laxative effects and also helps with gastric troubles.

COSMETICS:

A rinse containing rhubarb roots lightens blond hair. To prepare it, boil a handful of chopped roots in 1 cup water for 15 minutes. After it cools, strain the mixture and use it to rinse your hair. This mixture is not recommended for dark hair.

AN IMPORTANT PRECAUTION:

The leaves of common rhubarb must not be used in cooking because they contain a lot of toxic oxalic acid. Pregnant women should avoid eating rhubarb.

DECORATIVE USES:

Rhubarb is an imposing plant when grown in vegetables beds. The red-stalked types are especially attractive.

Rosmarinus officinalis
Rosemary

Type:

Location for growth:

Use:

Features:
!

FAMILY: Labiate family (*Lamiaceae*)

ORIGIN: Rosemary comes from the Mediterranean, where it often grows wild along the seashore. The ancient Romans and Greeks believed that rosemary brought good luck and protected people from evil spirits. Nowadays, Mediterranean cuisine would be sorely lacking without rosemary.

FEATURES: The shrub may grow up to 6 feet tall in its place of origin, but in northern latitudes it mostly stays smaller. It is generally not frost resistant. The needle-shaped leaves, which are gray on the bottom, are a characteristic feature of the plant. In spring it has light blue, white, or pink flowers. The aromatic leaves contain a lot of camphor-rich essential oil. The plant also contains saponins that have an expectorant effect, as well as tannins and bitter alkaloids.

TIP FOR THE SPECIES: "Blauer Toskaner" and "Benenden Blue" have bright blue flowers, while "Majorcan Pink" and "Roseus" have pink, and "Albiflorus" white. "Prostatus" is a creeper, "Severn Sea" has overhanging branches, and "Arp" and "Veitshöchheim" are known for their resistance to frost.

LOCATION FOR GROWTH: Because of its Mediterranean origin, rosemary loves a sunny and warm place. The ideal soil should contain humus and sand, and should be well tilled.

CULTIVATION: If you want to harvest rosemary as early as possible, buy a small plant in spring. Since many types of rosemary are not frost resistant, they are often grown in pots. In warmer regions rosemary can be planted in a protected place, but in winter it should be covered well. The shrub tolerates dry conditions better than extreme wetness; otherwise it is an easy plant to grow. In summer you can take cuttings, which root quite quickly. In winter keep the plant in a well-lit place at a temperature of 104 – 122°F and water only sparingly. In spring it is advisable to cut the plant back.

HARVEST: Leaves and buds can be harvested throughout the year and are used fresh. The stalks and leaves can be dried without losing their aroma. However, cut the plants back with care so that they do not lose too much of their beauty.

A SPECIAL TIP:

POTATOES WITH ROSEMARY

Use young, small potatoes and clean them well. Put them together with whole, unpeeled garlic cloves, fresh rosemary branches, and some ground pepper in a baking pan or baking bowl. Season the mixture with sea salt and drizzle with olive oil. Place in the oven and bake for 1½ to 2 hours at 650°F. These potatoes taste especially good with grilled meats, but can be also eaten with a dip.

USE:

CUISINE:

Thanks to its intense flavor, rosemary is a fine seasoning for meat, poultry, or fish. It also goes well with summer vegetable dishes. It is easy to prepare rosemary oil or vinegar - simply put a branch in the liquid and allow to sit for some time, then remove.

HEALTH EFFECTS:

Rosemary is good for the digestion as well as the blood circulation. Due to this effect, it is used as a basic ingredient in ointments for treating rheumatism. The plant also stimulates and strengthens the nerves.

COSMETICS:

Rosemary oil is a valuable base ingredient in perfumes and cosmetics. Added to bathwater, it has stimulating effects. To prepare a bath put 2 ounces rosemary leaves in boiling water, steep for 30 minutes, strain and then add to the bath.

DECORATIVE USES:

Rosemary has a pleasing scent and should be placed near a place where you like to relax.

IMPORTANT PRECAUTION:

Pregnant women should avoid rosemary because it stimulates the reproductive organs.

Rumex acetosa
Sorrel

<table>
<tr><td>

Type:

⊙

Location for growth:

Use:

Features:

❗

</td></tr>
</table>

FAMILY: Buckwheat family (*Polygonaceae*)

ORIGIN: Great sorrel is a European perennial that grows mainly in wet meadows and near water. The wild plant was familiar to the ancient Greeks. Large-leafed garden sorrel (*Rumex rugosus*, sooner *R. acetosa* var. *hortensis*) was cultivated from the wild plant and now is grown mostly in vegetable and herb gardens.

FEATURES: From the strong spreading roots of the plant, a stalk with file-like leaves rises in spring. The leaves of some types are 8 - 12 inches long and contain a lot of oxalic acid, vitamin C and iron. Tannins and alkaloids give the herb a sour, astringent taste. In early summer, the plant produces small, red flowers that sprout from red stalks in panicles.

TIP FOR SPECIES: Large-leafed "Belleville" is widely known. "Profusion" produces large, smooth leaves nearly all year round. However, it does not flower and can be obtained only in the form of a young plant.

SIMILAR SPECIES: Broad-leaved dock (*Rumex obtusifolius*) grows wild in Europe and can be used in cooking the same way as its relative is. Bloodwort (*R. sanguineus*) is very decorative, thanks to its leaves with small red veins, while French sorrel (*R. scutatus*) is somewhat smaller than garden sorrel, and grows best in pots and balcony boxes. It also exists in a silver-leafed form. Herb patience (*R. patienta*) contains less oxalic acid than any other type.

LOCATION FOR GROWTH: The plant prefers shade or partial shade, such as bordering woody plants. Grown in a sunny place, the plant produces rougher leaves. Well-tilled soil rich in humus is very important for the leaves to become juicy.

CULTIVATION: Sorrel can be sown directly in beds, in spring or summer. As sorrel grows rampantly it should not be sown too densely, otherwise you will have to thin the plants. Sorrel can also be obtained as a young plant, or you can easily divide larger plants. It must always be well watered. The leaves get stronger if you cut off the blossom umbels, which at the same time ensures that the plant will not propagate itself. It is recommended to renew sorrel plants every 3 – 5 years.

HARVEST: Young, smooth leaves – which can be frozen – are the best. The inner heartleaves should be left alone, so that the plant can quickly grow back.

A SPECIAL TIP

SORREL WITH VEGETABLES
Saute 2 chopped onions in 2 teaspoons olive oil. Wash a pound of sorrel leaves and 1 head of lettuce cut into strips, then peel 3 cloves of garlic and mash with salt. Add all the ingredients to the onions, and season to taste with salt and pepper. Cover and put in the oven for 10 minutes at medium temperature. Mix 3 egg yolks with 4 tablespoonfuls cream and add to the vegetables.

USE:

CUISINE:
Sorrel leaves, both raw and boiled, are used in soups, salads, and Frankfurter Green Sauce (see page 256 for recipe). They can be sautéed in butter, and when mixed with cream and egg yolks they create a rich vegetable side dish.

Schildzuring

HEALTH EFFECTS:
When taken in small doses sorrel cleanses the blood and supports digestion. In homeopathy it is used against colds, and against gastric and intestinal ailments.

DECORATIVE USES:
Sorrel does well in shady shrub gardens. Bloodwort, with its red veins, is especially decorative.

IMPORTANT PRECAUTION:

Children and people who are susceptible may suffer from vomiting or diarrhea after ingesting sorrel. This is caused by the high oxalic acid content. Sorrel tea (2 teaspoons of the plant in 1 cup of water) can relieve the symptoms of rheumatism and arthritis; however, no more than 2 cups should be consumed in a day.

Ruta graveolens
Rue

FAMILY: Rue family (*Rutaceae*)

ORIGIN: Rue is a typical plant of the Mediterranean, where it has been grown as an aromatic plant and an herb for centuries. Monks brought the plant to northern Europe, where it was used to treat eye ailments during the Middle Ages and thus was also called "eye rue." The plant was successfully used against plague, as its scent repelled disease-carrying rats.

FEATURES: This shrub, also called herb-of-grace, grows vertically to 20 - 30 inches and has only a few branches. Its blue-green leaves are feathery and smell like wine - if you hold them up to the light you can see many oil glands. In summer, the plant produces yellow flowers in panicles that grow from the ends of the branches. The plant contains a rich essential oil, the aromatic substance cumarin, alkaloids, tannins, and resins.

TIP FOR SPECIES: "Jackman's Blue" grows more compactly than the other types and has intense, blue-green leaves.

LOCATION FOR GROWTH: Rue grows best in a dry, sunny place. The soil can be rocky and poor, but it should be well tilled.

CULTIVATION: For domestic use, one plant is sufficient. You can buy it at your garden center, and later you can separate it or propagate it with cuttings. Sowing is also possible, but time-consuming. Once established in your garden, rue reseeds itself. Give the plant enough space – spacing of 12 to 16 inches is recommended. In colder areas rue should be covered for the winter. If you cut the shrub back in spring to 4 - 8 inches, it will produce a lot of branches.

HARVEST: The bitter, aromatic leaves can be harvested and used fresh all summer and most of the winter too. They also keep their aroma when dried or stored in oil. Since rue has an intense flavor you will need only small amounts.

A SPECIAL TIP:

SOOTHING TEA

This recommended tea contains a mix of herbs. Mix 10 parts rue and valerian, 15 parts lemon balm, mistletoe and whitethorn flowers as well as 5 parts caraway. Put 2 teaspoons of the mixture into 1 cup hot water and let it steep for 10 hours. Drink no more than 2 – 3 cups a day. If you want to prepare pure rue tea, put 1 teaspoon of the leaves into 1 cup of boiling water and strain after 5 minutes. Because of its side effects you should drink no more than 2 cups a day.

USE:

CUISINE:

Chopped rue can be added to herbal salads and sauces. It gives a special flavor to lamb, poultry, and pastas, and also tastes good with cheese. The classic dish "Hamburger Aalsuppe" (Hamburger eel soup) would not be possible without rue - neither would grappa.

HEALTH EFFECTS:

Rue dilates blood vessels, which is why it helps with headaches if you apply it near your eyes. The tea also helps with irregular menstruation and eases cramps. When using tea or homeopathic preparations, be careful not to exceed the recommended dose.

COSMETICS:

The essential oil in rue serves as the base for some perfumes. Rue sachets in your wardrobe repel moths.

DECORATIVE USES:

Rue is a very attractive plant thanks to its sparkly yellow blossoms and gray-green leaves. It looks especially good in rock gardens, where it repels dogs, cats and evil spirits with its smell.

IMPORTANT PRECAUTION:

Susceptible people may develop rashes after touching the plant, especially in the sun. Exceeding recommended doses may induce abortion, so pregnant women should avoid using rue.

Salvia officinalis
Sage

Type:
☉

Location for growth:
☼

Use:
✕ 🜲 ♈ ❀

Features:
!

FAMILY: Labiate family (*Lamiaceae*)

ORIGIN: True sage comes from the Mediterranean, where it grows predominantly in coastal areas. It has been known as a culinary and medicinal herb in northern Europe for centuries. In an herbal encyclopedia dating back to the 10th century you can read the following inscription: "When sage grows in gardens, why do people die of diseases?"

FEATURES: This evergreen, slightly woody shrub can grow up to 24 inches tall. Oblong, gray-green, velvety, hairy leaves with an intense aroma are typical of sage. In summer the plant produces violet-blue flowers in thick spikes. The leaves are rich in essential oil with camphor, tannins and alkaloids, as well as the expectorant saponin.

TIP FOR SPECIES: The species with leaves of various colors are especially fetching. The green leaves of "Icterina" have yellow spots, while the leaves of "Tricolor" are green, white and pink. "Purpurascens" has dark red leaves that contain valuable substances.

SIMILAR SPECIES: Clary sage (*Salvia sclarea*) gives off an intense musky odor. It is suitable for use in aromatic bouquets and herbal pillows, and also gives wines, marmalades, and stewed fruit a special flavor. Also, sage is a Common ingredient in perfumes and cosmetics for men because its smell is supposed to attract women.

LOCATION FOR GROWTH: This Mediterranean plant loves a warm, sunny place. The ground should be dry and well tilled.

CULTIVATION: Sage can be propagated by sowing; however, it is easier to buy a young plant in spring. The advantage of this is that you can choose from the assortment of different species and types. Bigger plants can be separated later. Unlike clary sage, true sage is cut back in spring so that it can easily grow back. In winter it should be covered.

HARVEST: Young leaves can be picked until fall. For drying, the stalks should be cut off before the plant blooms. Sage is its most aromatic in its second year.

A SPECIAL TIP:

SAGE MARINADE FOR GRILLING

Cut off the leaves from 3 stems of sage and mix together with 1 ground garlic clove, the peel and juice of 1 lemon, 3 spoonfuls olive oil, salt and pepper. Spread the marinade over the meat (such as lamb chops), leave in a cold place for at least 2 hours and then grill. Before grilling, the meat must be well drained.

Alternatively, sage leaves sautéed in oil and butter taste good with noodles.

USE:

CUISINE:
The leaves have an intense smell and should be used with care. They can be added to soups, meats, and fish, and should be cooked only briefly. Sage is an ingredient in Italian herb blends.

HEALTH EFFECTS:
Sage stimulates gall-bladder activity and makes heavy dishes more digestible. It also has antiseptic, disinfectant properties and heals wounds. Sage tea can be gargled to treat a sore throat and also supports milk flow in nursing mothers.

COSMETICS:
Sage leaves in baths relieve inflammation and help clean the skin.

DECORATIVE USES:
Flowering sage attracts lots of bees and butterflies. It looks great when grown in vegetable and herb gardens or rockeries. It also grows well in pots. The colored-leaf types are especially decorative.

IMPORTANT PRECAUTION:

Sage contains a poisonous substance – thujone – and when used in large doses it may be toxic. You should not drink more than 2 – 3 cups of sage tea a day. Pregnant women should avoid ingesting sage tea and oil.

Sanguisorba minor
Salad burnet

Type:
⊙

Location for growth:
☼ – ☀

Use:
✗ 𝕬

FAMILY: Rose family (*Rosaceae*)

ORIGIN: Salad burnet probably comes from the Mediterranean area, but it also grows wild in Central Europe in dry meadows and along roadsides. It has been cultivated in gardens as an herb and vegetable since the 16th century.

FEATURES: This perennial, hardy shrub grows up to 16 inches in height. Thick rosettes with long spiked leaves grow from strong, long roots, and the light-green fronds consist of 17 feathery leaves. The reddish-green flowers appear in thick spikes from May to June. The plant has a pleasant aroma.

SIMILAR SPECIES: Great burnet (*Sanguisorba officinalis*) is nearly 3 feet tall and produces small, reddish-brown flowers. It is used in cooking too, but is less popular because of its stickiness. It was once used as a blood-clotting agent because of its tannin content, but nowadays it is used as a gargle for mouth infections and for treating varicose veins.

LOCATION FOR GROWTH: Salad burnet prefers loose soil containing calcium, and loves full sun. It also grows well in partial shade. The plant tolerates dry conditions better than extreme dampness.

CULTIVATION: Salad burnet seeds are sown directly outdoors, spaced 12 inches apart, in spring or early summer. The plant can also be propagated by dividing an older specimen. For natural propagation, you must let the seed heads mature and then allow the seeds to spread in the wind, but for lush leaf growth it is recommended that you cut off the flowers - including the seed heads - during the summer.

HARVEST: The leaves can be harvested from May to November. They should be picked fresh and added to dishes. When dried the plant loses its delicious aroma. However, it is possible to freeze fresh leaves.

A SPECIAL TIP:

FRANKFURTER GREEN SAUCE

Salad burnet is a basic ingredient of this Frankfurt specialty. There are many recipes for green sauce; the following is from our grandmothers' time:

With a whisk blend 2 egg yolks with 2 spoonfuls mustard, 8 spoonfuls olive oil and 2 spoonfuls vinegar. Then add half a pint of sour cream, 4 ounces chopped herbs (salad burnet, parsley, chives, chervil, sorrel, borage, water cress) and 2 chopped hard-boiled eggs. Serve with potatoes.

USE:

CUISINE:

Salad burnet leaves have a piquant, spicy, slightly nutty, refreshing flavor, reminiscent of cucumber. The leaves shoold be sprinkled fresh over dishes since they lose their aroma when boiled. The taste goes best with eggs, cottage cheese, stewed fish, potatoes and vegetables. Salad burnet may also be added to salads and tastes good with bread and butter. It may be preserved in oil or vinegar, and preserving in salt is also possible, especially if the herb is mixed with parsley, dill or tarragon.

HEALTH EFFECTS:

Salad burnet has blood-cleansing properties and improves digestion thanks to its tannin content. It also strengthens heart activity. Salad burnet played an important role during the plague and other epidemics such as cholera and many stories about its healing properties can be heard to this day. However, it no longer plays such a great role, and is used less often.

Satureja montana
Winter savory

Type:

Location for growth:
☼

Use:

FAMILY: Labiate family (*Lamiaceae*)

ORIGIN: Originally from southern Europe, winter savory has been known for a long time. In the 9th century, the Benedictine monks brought it from the Mediterranean across the Alps.

FEATURES: This winter-hardy shrub, which grows to nearly 25 inches tall, produces thin, pointed, gray-green leaves. Its small lavender-pink to purple flowers bloom from June to September. They grow vertically in thick spikes and attract bees.

SIMILAR SPECIES: Annual summer savory (*Satureja hortensis*), with white or pink flowers, has a slightly peppery taste that goes especially well with fresh green beans and butter beans.

LOCATION FOR GROWTH: Winter savory is not especially demanding, but should be grown in soil with a low calcium content and in a warm, sunny place. Grown outdoors the plants should be covered in northern winters.

CULTIVATION: Winter savory is propagated mainly by sowing, and only rarely by dividing. Sow in April or May and plant outdoors in August. The seeds should be lightly covered with soil and spaced 12 inches apart. Cut back the stalks to the height of a hand in the spring.

HARVEST: The leaves and young stalks should be harvested just shortly before blooming as they lose their full aroma later. Cut the herb above the ground and hang in bundles to dry.

A special tip:

Winter savory tea
Add 3 teaspoons dried or fresh leaves to 1 cup boiling water
and allow to steep for 10 minutes, then strain and drink the
tea as hot as possible.

USE

CUISINE:

This spice - which smells strongly of beans - can be used fresh or dried and improves the taste of bean dishes, salads, and stews. It also gives a special flavor to tomato sauces and marinades for grilling. The stalks are boiled whole, whereas young leaves are added to dishes just before serving, whole or chopped. Winter savory goes very well with sage, rosemary, garlic, onions, and parsley, and can also be used for aromatic oils. To prepare such oil put 3 branches of the herb in a bottle with 1 cup vegetable oil (olive, sunflower, or peanut oil), close the bottles and let sit in a warm place for 1 week. Then strain, pour into clean bottles, and store in a cold place. Herbal tea made from dried winter savory improves your appetite, reduces flatulence, releases phlegm and helps subdue coughs. Sweeten the tea with honey.

HEALTH EFFECTS:

Winter savory contains essential oil and tannins. In the Middle Ages it was used as a universal cure, and nowadays it is used to assist digestion, relieve flatulence and cramps, and kill germs. It can be used for treating insect stings - apply it in paste form.

Sedum reflexum
Blue stonecrop

Type:

Location for
growth:

☼

Use:

FAMILY: *Crassulaceae*

ORIGIN: Blue stonecrop, also known by the name Sedum
rupestre, was in past centuries one of the most widely grown
plants in herb gardens, believed in the Middle Ages to have
magical powers. The plant grows wild in dry, rocky places
or in sandy soil. During dry periods it stores liquid in its succulent needles.

FEATURES: This evergreen shrub, which grows to 4 inches
tall, produces sturdy, green- or blue- striped shoots that lie
on the ground. Its pointed, blue-green or occasionally red
needles are thick and give the plant its French name, which
means something like "fat madam." Small, yellow flowers
bloom from June to August.

SIMILAR SPECIES: Gold-moss (*Sedum acre*) grows wild not
only in Europe but also in Turkey and northern Africa. Its
growth and flowers are similar to those of blue stonecrop. Its
star-shaped, yellow-green flowers appear in the summer, and
it has egg-shaped needles that have a sharp taste and beneficial effects on health. The plant was used as early as the

time of Hippocrates, who applied it to swellings and inflammations. White stonecrop (*S. album*), which grows up to 5 feet tall, has blunt needles and white flowers.

LOCATION FOR GROWTH: This unpretentious, succulent perennial grows best in sandy soil with good sun. Thanks to its growth characteristics it is especially suitable for rockeries and borders.

CULTIVATION: This plant can be easily grown in a garden. The seeds should be germinated indoors in early spring or sown directly outdoors, and should be strewn over the soil - not covered. It is easier to obtain a divided plant or a seedling from your garden center. In early summer you can take cuttings from plants that have not bloomed yet. The cuttings will root quickly. The plants require spacing of about 6 inches and should be watered with care – neither too much nor too little.

HARVEST: The spiny, pointed, gray-green needles and the stalk tops of non-blooming plants can be harvested all year. They are not suitable for drying because of their fleshy nature, but you can store them frozen.

A SPECIAL TIP:

NEW POTATOES
Put fresh chopped blue stonecrop needles in melted butter and pour over new potatoes. The aroma is not very strong so you can use a lot.

Use:

Cuisine:
Freshly harvested needles have a refreshing, sour flavor with a slightly bitter aroma. Coarsely chopped, they can be added to salads and herbal dressings, and are used to season vegetables and sauces.

Health effects:
Blue spruce contains alkaloids which reduce high blood pressure and the hardening of blood vessels. Traditionally, the leaves were used to treat hemorrhoids and relieve the pain of skin inflammations.

Sinapsis alba
Mustard

FAMILY: Mustard family (*Brassicaceae*)

ORIGIN: White mustard originally came from the Mediterranean, Asia and eastern India. It is one of the ancient plants mentioned in the Bible, and was brought across the Alps by the Romans to be grown in monastery gardens. Since that time, the mustard produced from the plant's seeds has become a basic ingredients in Western cuisine. Nowadays white mustard also grows wild.

FEATURES: This annual grows up to 4 feet tall and produces almost horizontal pods, which stand away from the stalks. The seeds are yellowish-white, and give the plant its name. Small bristles grow on the stalks and the divided, feathered leaves. Clusters of light yellow flowers appear in summer.

SIMILAR SPECIES: Black mustard (*Brassica nigra*) has a growth pattern and appearance similar to that of white mustard. However, it grows a little taller and its pods are parallel to each other. The black seeds have a spicier, more intense flavor.

LOCATION FOR GROWTH: White mustard is an easy plant to grow. It prefers dry, sunny places and grows best in soil containing calcium, humus, sand, and clay. It does not tolerate other members of the mustard family, such as cabbage, so it should not be grown together with them.

CULTIVATION: Seeds should be germinated from spring to early summer in pots or be sown directly in beds, spaced about 8 inches apart in a warm, sunny place. Young plants grow quite slowly and must be regularly weeded. Fertilizing will make them grow more vigorously.

HARVEST: In summer, the seeds are ready for harvest as soon as the pods turn yellow. For the highest yield, cut the plants back to just above the ground, tie them into small bundles, and hang them to dry. Store the seeds in a dark place until fully dry and turn them regularly. When the seeds are fully dry, store in sealed bottles. Young leaves should be harvested before the flowers open.

A SPECIAL TIP:

MUSTARD COMPRESS

This mustard compress used to be the most effective home remedy for severe bronchitis, and was used before antibiotics existed. To prepare the compress, crush 1 handful mustard seeds in a mortar. Add 4 spoonfuls warm water and let sit for a short time until the mixture releases a sharp mustard oil aroma. Soak a towel in the liquid, put it on the chest and cover with a wool scarf or some similar material. Remove after 20 minutes.

USE:

CUISINE:

White mustard is a universal spice that is used in many dishes and naturally tastes good with all kinds of sausages. It also improves the taste of many cold and hot sauces and goes well with ginger, lemon, and onions. The seeds are used either whole or ground, and provide the base for American table mustard and Bavarian sweet mustard. Young, fresh mustard leaves can be prepared as a tasty salad.

HEALTH EFFECTS:

Mustard seeds are about one-third oil. They also contain albumen and sinalbin (a glucoside) - the latter is responsible for the sharp taste of mustard. Mustard supports digestion and the metabolism, activates body circulation, and heals mouth irritations.

Solidago virgaurea
Goldenrod

FAMILY: Daisy family (*Asteraceae*)

ORIGIN: Common goldenrod grows on river banks as well as along roadsides. It may have been used to treat wounds. It also has diuretic properties.

FEATURES: This frost-resistant shrub grows up to 3 feet high. It produces pointed alternating leaves. From late summer to early fall the plant produces small golden-yellow flower heads in panicles. Goldenrod is rich in essential oil, tannins, dyes, and flavonoids as well as citric and oxalic acids.

LOCATION FOR GROWTH: Robust goldenrod prefers full sun but also grows well in partial shade. Ideally, soil should be sandy, fertile, and well-tilled. It can be grown in shrub borders together with wood avens, agrimony, or bee balm. It also thrives in rockeries with wet soil.

CULTIVATION: Goldenrod can be propagated by dividing in spring or fall. You can also obtain seeds or young plants at your garden center. If you want to keep the plant from reseeding itself, cut off the shoots after it blooms. Goldenrod

survives winter outdoors without any problems, but is often attacked by aphids and mildew.

HARVEST: The shoot's tops contain a lot of diuretic substances, and can be harvested from July to September. The plant can be dried and prepared as a tea.

A SPECIAL TIP:

GOLDENROD TEA BLEND

You can prepare a tea blend that helps with gout by increasing secretion of water. To prepare the tea mix 1 ounce goldenrod, and half an ounce each birch leaves, dandelion roots, spiny restharrow roots and peppermint leaves. Pour 1 heaping teaspoon of the mixture into 1 cup of boiling water, let it steep, and then strain. Drink 2 cups a day for about 3 – 4 weeks.

USE

HEALTH EFFECTS:
The plant stimulates kidney activity, relieves problems associated with kidney diseases, and heals blisters. Thanks to its diuretic effects it can also be used to treat rheumatism and skin swellings. However, goldenrod should not be used in heavy or extended doses if water retention is due to limited heart or kidney activity. Cold goldenrod tea helps with tonsillitis when gargled.

COSMETICS:
Goldenrod is used as a dye because it contains a lot of pigment.

DECORATIVE USES:
Goldenrod is grown in gardens for its bright, attractive blossom heads. It can also be used in bouquets.

IMPORTANT PRECAUTION:

Goldenrod pollen is partly responsible for hay fever. If you suffer from chronic kidney disease consult your doctor before using it.

Tanacetum parthenium
Feverfew

Type:
⊙ – ∞

Location for
growth:
☼ – ☀

Use:
♠ ♈ ❀

Features:
!

FAMILY: Daisy family (*Asteraceae*)

ORIGIN: This short-lived shrub originally came from the Caucasus but became widespread as an herb and decorative plant in other parts of Europe. Feverfew was used in past centuries mainly against childbed fever, and to induce labor.

FEATURES: This annual or perennial, which may grow up to 20 inches in height, has egg-shaped, hairy fronds that consist of three to five pairs of small leaves. In summer the plant produces flowers reminiscent of daisies, with yellow centres and white "petals".

TIP FOR SPECIES: From the basic feverfew, many new types and forms have been cultivated. "Aureum" has golden-yellow leaves and simple, yellow, overhanging white flower heads. "Butterball" (which grows up to 7 inches tall) produces full, yellow flowers, while "Ball's Double White" has full, white flower heads. "Golden Moss" (a dwarf variety) produces small pillow blooms in white, and white "Santana" has aigrette blossoms.

SIMILAR SPECIES: For laymen it is difficult to see any difference between feverfew and alecost (*Tanacetum balsamita*). Alecost grows up to 3 feet tall and produces smaller, bright whitish-yellow flowers. In gardens it is cultivated for its leaves, which smell like balm. Alecost was used as early as the 14th century as a spice for soups and a treatment for wounds. At 5 feet tall, tansy (*T. vulgare*) produces golden-yellow flower heads. Its strong smell makes it a natural insect repellent, and when taken internally it kills worms. It also helps to regulate menstruation. Since the 9th century it has been used to season fish, liqueurs, and sausages.

LOCATION FOR GROWTH: Feverfew thrives in any type of soil if it is not too wet or hard. It prefers full sun but also grows well in partial shade.

CULTIVATION: Feverfew is usually grown from seeds. It is best to germinate the seeds indoors and plant outdoors in April. Depending on the type, the plant may reseed itself. Feverfew can also be propagated by dividing or with cuttings. It is especially well suited for pots.

HARVEST: The leaves may be harvested and used fresh or dried.

A SPECIAL TIP:

FEVERFEW BODY LOTION
Boil 1 full handful feverfew leaves in half a pint of milk. Allow to cool and strain, pour into clean bottles, and store in a cold place. This milk lubricates dry skin and prevents blisters.

USE:

HEALTH EFFECTS:

Feverfew contains essential oils and alkaloids. It was once prepared as a bitter tea to induce labor. The healing powers of this old home remedy have been confirmed and the plant is recommended for headaches and migraines. Sachets of dried leaves placed in wardrobes repel moths.

COSMETICS:

Feverfew can be spread over the skin, soothing it with its active substances.

DECORATIVE USES:

Thanks to its pretty flowers, feverfew looks great not only in groups grown in gardens but also in pots on your balcony or terrace.

Boerenwormkruid

IMPORTANT PRECAUTION:

As feverfew also contains toxic substances it should be used with care. Pregnant women should avoid its use. Tansy is not recommended for home use because of its high content of toxic substances.

Taraxacum officinale
Common dandelion

FAMILY: Daisy family (*Asteraceae*)

ORIGIN: This wild plant, which originated in Europe, has spread over the whole northern hemisphere, where it grows mainly in meadows. Its healthful effects were already known to the ancient Arabs and Greeks. The Middle Ages were the golden age for this plant. In France it is called "Pissenlit" because of its diuretic effects.

FEATURES: The 8 - 16 inch stalks with long jagged leaves that grow in the form of rosettes are typical for this plant. In spring the plant produces hollow, smooth stalks and glistening yellow flowers from which its seed heads develop. Common dandelions are popular with children. The plant contains white, non-poisonous milky sap and is rich in minerals, vitamin C, iron, and silicic acid, as well as tannins and alkaloids.

TIP FOR SPECIES: There are special types of dandelion with many leaves that have been cultivated for vegetable gardens and taste less bitter. They are "Vollherziger," "Lyonel" and "Nouvelle" - the latter two are also suitable for growing in winter.

LOCATION FOR GROWTH: The common dandelion is an easy plant to grow and prefers full sun or partial shade. It requires rich, deep, loose soil.

CULTIVATION: The best time for sowing comes from the middle to end of May. Sow in rows spaced 10 – 12 inches apart; thin the seedlings later to the same spacing. It is important to water and mow them regularly. Should the common dandelion not reseed itself, spread the seeds by hand. In winter, growth can be accelerated as follows: dig up the plant in fall, cut off the stalks a few centimeters above the roots and plant in a box or big pot with well aerated soil. Then cover the box or pots with an opaque lid and store at a temperature of 60 - 65°F for 3 – 4 weeks.

HARVEST: Young leaves are usually cut off right above the ground, but the heart of the plant should not be damaged. The "summer leaves" have a slightly bitter taste, while the pale "winter leaves" are smooth and mild. When stored in a closed box in the refrigerator, they stay fresh for about 1 week. Besides the leaves, you can also use the roots and buds in cooking. Flowers, stalks, and sap are popular in various therapies. Should you want to use dandelions picked from the wild, make sure you do not gather those growing on roadsides or in fertilized fields.

A SPECIAL TIP:

POWER COCKTAIL

Make a purée from 1 handful common dandelion leaves, 1 orange and 1 cored apple. Sweeten with honey to taste and add half a pint of juice or buttermilk. Drink a glass a day and spring may arrive sooner!

Use:

CUISINE:

Raw dandelion leaves are a vitamin-rich base for salads, and can be served with potatoes or eggs. They can also be sautéed like vegetables. The roots can be dug up in spring or fall, cut into small pieces, roasted in the oven (10 – 15 minutes at 450 – 480°F), and then ground, giving you a caffeine-free substitute for coffee.

HEALTH EFFECTS:

Dandelions have diuretic and blood-cleansing effects, and are a great way to detox! Fresh stalks eaten for about 2 weeks help, as do tea and juice, with skin rashes, kidney stones, diabetes, and rheumatism. To prepare 1 cup of tea, use 1 tablespoonful roots and leaves.

DECORATIVE USES:

Dandelions enrich a natural garden layout thanks to their bright, pretty, yellow blossoms, which attract bees.

IMPORTANT PRECAUTION:

Susceptible people may suffer allergic reactions to dandelions. If you suffer from gastritis, intestinal disease or gall-bladder disease, consult your doctor before use. The milky sap is not poisonous, but it leaves brown spots on clothes and skin.

Thymus vulgaris
Thyme

Type:

⊙

Location for growth:

☼

Use:

✗

FAMILY: Labiate family (*Lamiaceae*)

ORIGIN: True thyme originally came from the Mediterranean area and northern and western Africa. Egyptians, Greeks and Romans appreciated its health benefits. It was grown as a therapeutic and culinary herb in monastery gardens in the Middle Ages.

FEATURES: This shrub (which grows to 12 – 16 inches tall) has many light, woody branches. Its thin, tough leaves are slightly rolled at the tips and have a needle-like shape. From June to August, the plant produces small white, pink or violet whorled flowers.

SIMILAR SPECIES: Lemon thyme (*Thymus citriodorus*) (a hybrid of coconut thyme (*T. pulegioides*) and true thyme) smells and tastes like grapefruit and is used in salads. It produces pale, lavender-colored flowers while other types such as "Aureus" and "Golden King" have golden-yellow flowers.

LOCATION FOR GROWTH: Thyme requires full sun and dry, well-tilled soil. It needs no fertilizer besides some compost.

CULTIVATION: Since thyme germinates in the light, the seeds should be covered with only a little soil. Starting in May they can be sown directly outdoors. Plant seedlings in the spring, spaced 8 inches apart. You can take cuttings from older plants in the summer, and if you cut the plant back regularly in summer or spring it quickly produces new, smooth stalks. True thyme is frost-resistant. If the ground is wet, hibernation may be affected.

Harvest: The leaves and young stems can be harvested from May to November. To dry the plants, cut them shortly before they bloom and hang in a shady, airy place.

A special tip:

Thyme bath lotion
You can make a thyme steam bath, which will help if you suffer from infections of the airways, sinus inflammations or skin problems. Put 2 handfuls fresh thyme leaves and flowers in a bowl, add a quart of boiling water and let sit for some time. Cover your head with a towel and keep your head over the bowl for 10 minutes. Then wash your face with cold water and dry it.

USE

CUISINE:

Whether it is used fresh or dried, thyme's pleasant, spicy-sweet taste goes especially well with Mediterranean dishes, giving a special flavor to lamb in particular. Thyme is an important ingredient of "herbes de Provence." Thanks to its flatulence-easing properties, thyme makes heavy foods more digestible. It stands up to lengthy boiling better than many other herbs. Dried thyme leaves are, in general, stronger than fresh leaves.

HEALTH EFFECTS:

Thyme is rich in essential oils as well as phenol, thymol, and carvacrol, so it stimulates digestion, eases flatulence, and has antiseptic and calming effects. Prepared as a tea it helps relieve diarrhea, and it soothes inflammations of the mouth and pharynx, as well as coughs and bronchitis. Used in compress or lotion form thyme heals small wounds, bruises, and boils. When used in a bath, thyme oil helps with respiratory ailments, rheumatism, and general exhaustion.

Tropaeolum majus
Nasturtium

Type:

Location for growth:

Use:

Features:
!

FAMILY: Nasturtium family (*Tropaeolaceae*)

ORIGIN: Nasturtium originally came from the Andes area - Colombia, Ecuador, Peru, and Bolivia - where it grows at colder mountain elevations. In its home this decorative runner plant has long been appreciated for its antiseptic properties.

FEATURES: This frost-susceptible annual produces 9-foot tendrils. Its rounded or kidney-shaped, light green leaves are wavy at their tips. From summer to fall, the plant produces pretty orange or red blossoms.

TIP FOR SPECIES: Different types vary mainly in height and the color of the blossoms. "Peach Melba" has creamy-yellow flowers that are orange-red in the middle, and "Hermine Grasshof" flowers are light red. Besides the creeping types, there are also compactly growing varieties.

LOCATION FOR GROWTH: The plant prefers a sunny place in a garden, balcony, or terrace, but also grows well in partial

shade. Regular fertilizing and watering are important in summer, but over-watering should be avoided. Nasturtiums do not require a specific soil type, but rich soil, especially with a high nitrogen content, stimulates the growth of leaves instead of blossoms, which is why nitrogen-poor soil is recommended. Nasturtium can cover large areas or hang from pots.

CULTIVATION: Nasturtium is suitable for growing in garden herb beds as well as in pots or boxes on terraces or balconies. Grown together with fruit trees and cabbage, it repels aphids and caterpillars. This annual should not be sown outdoors before May because of its susceptibility to frost. In April it can be germinated indoors. It is best to sow 3 – 4 seeds in a small pot.

HARVEST: Even though nasturtium is grown as a decorative plant in gardens, it can be also used as a delicious cooking herb. Nearly all the plant's parts may be eaten - flowers, buds, and leaves. Young leaves are harvested from May to October and are used fresh, while the flowers are harvested during the blooming period.

A SPECIAL TIP:

SPICY PICKLED NASTURTIUM BUDS
Nasturium buds pickled in vinegar or salt are a delicious substitute for capers.

USE:

CUISINE:

The slightly bitter leaves with their mustardy taste can be added to salads, fresh cheese, cottage cheese, and omelets, to which they add a piquant flavor. Chopped, they improve the taste of sauces and vinaigrettes. The juicy younger leaves taste mild and are used whole or chopped, raw or lightly sautéed, and also as a garnish. Nasturtium goes with almost all spring herbs.

HEALTH EFFECTS:

The plant contains a lot of essential oils and in the Central and South American countries of its origin it is used to treat wounds. Thanks to its antiseptic properties it can also be used internally, for example for urinary tract inflammations. Nasturtium stimulates the appetite, has gentle secretory effects, and improves the body's immunity.

IMPORTANT PRECAUTION:

Nasturtium leaves should be used with care so as not to cause gastric or intestinal irritation.

Valeriana officinalis
Valerian

Type:

⊙

Location for
growth:

☼ – ☀

Use:

Features:

!

FAMILY: Valerian family (*Valerianaceae*)

ORIGIN: True valerian, also known as "garden heliotrope," grows all over the world. It prefers wet places, such as pond banks, meadows and forest borders. In the Middle Ages, it was used as a treatment for gout. Witches and demons were said to be repelled by it. The plant has been known for centuries for its calming effects and today, it is widely grown for pharmacological preparations.

FEATURES: This vertically-growing shrub, which can reach up to 6 feet tall, produces short, compact rhizomes. Fleshy branching shoots with light green, deeply feathered leaves grow from strong roots. From July to August, the plant produces umbels of white or pink blossoms. The plant contains alkaloids that have calming effects.

LOCATION FOR GROWTH: Valerian should be grown in gardens in full sun or partial shade and prefers wet soil. It is suitable for large home gardens, shrub boxes or herb gardens, but it requires plenty of space for its many shoots. In gardens with wild plants this shrub may propagate itself.

CULTIVATION: The shrub grows up to 6 feet tall and reaches a span of about 30 inches. Individual plants should therefore be spaced 16 inches apart, covered with plenty of compost, and kept damp. Valerian is started indoors in early spring and sown outdoors in the summer. You can also take cuttings from older plants, and in fall or spring you can divide older specimens. Loose, well-tilled soil that is not excessively wet is required for effective cultivation.

HARVEST: Valerian roots are the most health-giving part of the plant. You can cut roots from older shrubs in fall. Clean and wash under running water, cut into pieces and dry on strings or in the oven. Make sure you do not damage the plant too much when harvesting the roots.

A SPECIAL TIP:

VALERIAN BATH

Pour 1 quart boiling water over 4 ounces valerian root and let it sit for 10 hours. Then strain and add the liquid to your bath. Or something easier: add valerian tincture bought at the drugstore to your bath. The ideal temperature for the water is about 100 °F and the ideal bathing time is a maximum of 15 minutes.

USE:

HEALTH EFFECTS:

Valerian is successfully used against insomnia, nervousness, and stress. Its calming effects are caused by the chemical valepotriate. The plant also contains isovalerian acid, esters and tannins, as well as essential oils. During periods of nervousness or insomnia a valerian bath before bed should bring quick relaxation, but be careful – people have often fallen asleep in the tub! The plant is also believed to stimulate appetite. To prepare a cup of valerian tea pour boiling water over 1 – 2 teaspoons chopped roots. After 10 minutes the tea is ready.

> ### IMPORTANT PRECAUTION:
>
> **If you use valerian for extended periods or exceed the recommended dose, it can cause side-effects such as headache, faintness, and accelerated heartbeat.**

COSMETICS:

Valerian oil is also used industrially for perfumes and as an aromatic ingredient in foods and beverages.

DECORATIVE USES:

The plant produces many white or pink flowers. Dried, it can also be used in decorative bouquets.

Viola odorata
Violet

Type:

∞

Location for growth:

Use:

Features:

!

FAMILY: Violet family (*Violaceae*)

ORIGIN: The violet, also known as sweet violet, originally came from the Mediterranean area and is spread throughout Europe today. This small plant has many health benefits and was loved by the ancient Greeks. Athenians took it as their symbol and adorned their gods with violets.

FEATURES: This evergreen shrub produces vertical shoots with heart-shaped, jagged leaves. It has sweetly-scented purple, blue, red or white flowers about 1 inch wide which bloom in late winter or early spring. The plant contains saponins and essential oils, as well as dyes.

SIMILAR SPECIES: Johnny Jumpup or heartsease (*Viola tricolor*) grows wild all over Europe. It produces flowers of many colors - purple, lavender, blue, white, and yellow - and the lower crown leaves are often darkly striped. In medicine it is used against children's dermatitis, scabies, and other skin diseases. The shoots are used in ointments and pastes.

LOCATION FOR GROWTH: Johnny Jumpup grows best in well-fertilized, humus-rich soil, and prefers partial shade. The plant grows well in gardens with wild plants or scrubs.

CULTIVATION: This hardy violet reseeds itself easily in gardens or propagates itself by means of runners. If you want to propagate the plant yourself you can divide it in spring or fall. You can also purchase seeds at your local garden center and sow them outdoors. If you want to extend the blooming period, regularly pick off wilted flowers. This plant is often attacked by mosaic virus, rust, and mildew.

HARVEST: All parts of the violet, but especially the flowers and roots, can be harvested in spring for medicinal purposes.

Viola tricolor

A SPECIAL TIP

VIOLET COUGH SYRUP

Put about 1 cup fresh violet flowers into a bottle and pour in 1 cup hot water. Let sit for 24 hours and then strain. Then boil with the same amount of fresh violet blossoms and again let it sit for 24 hours. Strain again and add an equal amount of honey. Take one teaspoon several times a day.

Use:

Cuisine:
The violet's smooth, tender leaves add a special flavor to green salads, while its pretty, edible blossoms are used to garnish salads or desserts. In France the flowers are candied and eaten.

Health effects:
The plant contains the alkaloid violin as well as various saponins, and is used as a natural treatment for coughs, especially bronchitis and catarrh of the upper airways. It can also be used to relieve headaches, insomnia, and skin ailments, and is believed to have anti-cancer effects. To prepare tea, pour 1 cup boiling water over 1 teaspoon dried leaves and strain after 10 minutes. The recommended dose is 3 cups a day.

> Important precaution:
> **Excess violet root may cause vomiting.**

Cosmetics:
Violet flowers are used in perfume production.

Decorative uses:
Violets look very pretty in colored pots on window ledges or balconies.

Photographs by:

Roland Spohn: p. 23, 35, 39, 51, 55, 59, 67, 71, 75, 87, 91, 92, 103, 115, 127, 135, 171, 185, 187, 199, 203, 207, 211, 215, 227, 228, 231, 243, 245, 255, 260, 267, 269, 279, 281

Anette Timmermann: p. 9, 10, 11, 13, 14, 19, 31, 33, 43, 49, 60, 73, 76, 79, 83, 84, 107, 113, 119, 123, 128, 143, 151, 152, 161, 175, 179, 183, 195, 196, 221, 223, 233, 235, 239, 247, 251, 253, 259, 271, 272, 275, 283, 284, 287, 289, 291

Werner Rauh: p. 29, 47, 95, 99, 111, 139, 159, 163, 167, 191, 277, 295
Elvira Gross: p. 63, 131, 147, 155, 219, 263, 296

Brigitte Sporrer and Alena Hrbkova: p. 27, 36, 45, 52, 57, 101, 117, 164, 220, 225, 265

All data included in this encyclopedia has been included by the authors and checked by the publisher with care, according to their best conscience. At the same time – since we have to point this out because of the product law – possible mistakes cannot be eliminated. Therefore the data is published without any guarantee from the publisher or authors. None of the parties accept any responsibility for possible misunderstandings.